FINDING YOUR
PATH

THE ROADMAP FROM STUDENT TO
SUCCESSFUL FINANCIAL PLANNER

Caleb Brown, MBA, CFP®

**Dedicating this book to all New Financial Planners; I've got
your back!**

CONTENTS

—·—

FOREWORD

I had heard about Caleb long before I ever met him. As the saying goes, his reputation does precede him.

When we finally met in front of a bonfire at a conference, I got to see Caleb and learn more about what drove him—what still drives him. Caleb had just started New Planner Recruiting and was deeply concerned with making the path to a financial planning career easier for new financial planners. Over the bonfire crackle, we discussed and strategized about our shared dream of helping students and making a lasting impact on our profession.

Even before our first meeting, Caleb had already played an essential role in my career. In 2003, Caleb was a full-time financial planner and was also volunteering his time to start the FPA Dallas/Fort Worth Career Day. It was among the first financial planning career days in the country. Like many who came before and after me, it was at that event that I got my internship and my first full-time job.

Since that first fireside meeting, we've shared more conversations and worked to turn many of those dreams into reality. I am inspired by all that Caleb has accomplished—his impact on new and aspiring financial planners and firms. When you factor in the environment financial planning was in when Caleb started, it makes his story even more impressive.

Caleb's passion for financial planning career paths directly opposed a culture that prized the status quo. Naysayers asked, "Why do we need this? The way it's always been done is good enough." Caleb was one of the first to do something about creating new career paths for aspiring planners. He took his idea and crafted it into something tangible. And for that, he has earned respect and admiration from me and many others in our profession.

Within these pages, you will find a practical guide to join or sharpen your skills in financial planning. Caleb will be honest with you. He'll tell you when you're a weak candidate, but he won't stop there. He cares about you and will give you the roadmap and tools to become that strong candidate. Caleb offers insights that will shorten your learning curve, prepare you to succeed, and make a difference in your career.

Becoming a financial planner was the best choice I ever made. I am glad you're here and that you, too, are considering it. I'm excited that our profession has Caleb Brown in it. He continues to push forward to advocate for new financial planners and the firms they work for.

In short, Caleb is advocating for, believing in, and equipping you!

Hannah Moore
Founder, Guiding Wealth
Founder, Amplified Planning
Founder, Financial Planning Externship
www.amplifiedplanning.com

—·—

INTRODUCTION

C ongratulations on your decision to become a financial planner. You're about to embark on a fabulous journey unlike any other you may have taken before. In the pages to come, you'll find a detailed map for your quest for ultimate career success as a financial planner. This book is meant to serve as a guide to help you cut through the complexity and confusion so that you can accelerate your career growth and enjoy job satisfaction that is second to none.

Financial planning is more than retirement planning, investment management, or insurance. It's about relationships. It's about listening. It's about understanding your client's goals and dreams. It's about helping them make the best possible decisions to positively impact their financial and emotional well-being.

Our profession is not an old one. It's only about fifty years old. Although the investment and insurance vocations have been around much longer, they still pale compared to the more well-established professions such as law, medicine, and accounting. Unlike those, you are entering a profession you can help shape and mold for future generations. First, it's essential to understand our great profession's origin and see how far we've come in such a short time.

Beginnings

It began with Loren Dunton, who is considered the Father of Financial Planning. Loren was a career salesman who trained other salespeople facing a recession in the late 1960s and growing tired of seeing their compensation and livelihoods closely tied to an economy that experienced sharp peaks and valleys. He arranged a meeting with twelve of his peers in December of 1969 at the Chicago O'Hare Hilton to discuss how to create a new profession devoted to personal financial advice and not solely product sales. [1]

It was an idea that stemmed from his work with clients and a year-long trip worldwide. His travels helped him realize that Americans were not preparing well for retirement. Instead, they relied too heavily on Social Security and other government programs.[2]

He envisioned a new profession in the private sector that would provide ongoing advice to clients for all areas of their financial lives. These new financial advisers would approach the client's situation more holistically, which involved reviewing all areas of the client's financial situation versus insurance and investments only. The decisions from that meeting laid the groundwork for the financial planning profession as we know it today.

Today, the financial planning profession is strong and rapidly growing. According to the U.S. Bureau of Labor Statistics and other industry researchers, more than 300,000 financial advisors provide services to clients, and roughly 30,000 Registered Investment Advisor firms (RIAs), including those registered with the Securities Exchange

---

1. http://www.dunton.org/archive/biographies/loren_dunton/history_of_fp.htm

2. Interview with Page Lambert; daughter of Loren Dunton

Commission (SEC) and various state regulatory agencies.[3,4] An RIA is a company that registers with the appropriate governing bodies and provides investment advice to individuals or companies.

In 2021, the U.S. Bureau of Labor Statistics cited that the national median salary for a financial planner was about $90,000, more than twice the national average.[5] However, this can vary drastically depending on the amount of experience an advisor has, the size of the firm, and the firm location. It can range anywhere from $50,000 per year for someone just starting to $500,000 per year or more for those with experience that can bring in clients and/or own their businesses. Momentum for the financial planning profession is mounting, highlighted by the following three trends:

Trend #1

Highly profitable business model — Financial planning firms, especially the smaller independent solo practices, are typically highly profitable with profit margins in the 20%–30%+ range. Once a client base is developed, as long as the advisor continues to provide good service and does not lose clients, firms tend to grow rapidly, especially if the stock market increases. The challenge here, as we discuss later in the book, is that it might not be so straightforward to build up a client base, and it will not happen overnight, and the stock market does not perpetually go up either.

---

3. https://www.statista.com/statistics/614815/number-of-rias-employed-usa/

4. https://www.financial-planning.com/news/state-registered-rias-to-get-fee-guidance-from-nasaa

5. https://www.bls.gov/ooh/business-and-financial/personal-financial-advisors.htm

Trend #2

An explosion of technology solutions — As the financial planning profession has continued to evolve over the past several years, it has seen a sharp increase in the number of ancillary products and services available to support the growing number of financial planners.

Financial technology (fintech) companies have seized the opportunity to design software, develop apps, and introduce new platforms to assist financial planners in offering financial planning services to more clients without hiring more staff.

Thanks to these new technologies and the advent of "Robo-advisors" (a brokerage account that automatically rebalances), the profession has fully commoditized investment management services. It has allowed financial planners to better serve lower net-worth clients without sacrificing profits.

Many professionals were initially concerned when robo-advisors were first announced, and some even feared the robos would replace human advisors completely, but this has not come to fruition. Nor do I think it will. Currently, artificial intelligence (AI) applications such as ChatGPT have some financial planners fearful for their jobs, but similar to the robos, I don't see human advisors being replaced. Instead, adapting these technologies will help the financial planning profession provide services to more of the population that traditionally did not have access to financial planning because they did not have the required minimum income level and assets.

Trend #3

Innovation of new business models — Besides the standard Registered Investment Advisor (RIA) model, many other service platforms appear today. These range from virtual firms to financial coaching platforms, firms that offer planning services as corporate fringe benefit providers, firms that work exclusively with Generation X or Y clientele, and firms housed within banks and accounting firms.

***

We have a perfect storm brewing in the profession today, making it an attractive time to become a financial planner. In addition to the aging financial planner community (over half of all financial planners are over the age of 55),[6] there are an estimated 10,000 Americans from the baby boomer generation turning 65 each day.[7] These retiring boomers need a suite of financial planning services ranging from retirement planning to investment management, insurance selection, estate planning, and more.

Demographic research experts cite that great wealth transfer will pass an estimated $70 trillion from the older generations to the newer generations. Many younger investors do not have a relationship with a financial planner.[8]

It is also worth noting that the rise of subscription and other service fee (retainer, hourly, project, etc.) models make it possible for younger advisors to serve their peers. Hence, you aren't limited to only working with older retirees, as has been the primary focus for financial planners for the last few decades.

---

6. https://www.jdpower.com/business/press-releases/2019-us-financial-advisor-satisfaction-study

7. https://smartasset.com/retirement/baby-boomers-retiring

8. Dore, Kate. "Are You Prepared for Tax Impact of the $68 Trillion Great Wealth Transfer? Here Are Some Options to Reduce the Bite." CNBC.com, 12 July 2021

When you combine this influx of potential clients with the complex legislation that has recently passed, namely the Tax Cuts and Jobs Act, CARES Act, and Secure Act 2.0, it becomes apparent that more individuals need financial guidance and advice than ever before. A profession previously marred by the notion that it was only for the high-net-worth and ultra-wealthy has changed over the years due to constant innovation and challenging the status quo. Financial planning has now become accessible to Americans from all walks of life, creating growth and new opportunities within the profession.

So, why did I write this book?

Thus far in my career via our recruiting firm www.newplannerrec ruiting.com, I have spoken to over 10,000 job seekers about career opportunities within the financial planning profession and helped over 1,000 find their right career fit, spread out among over 500 financial planning firms nationwide. We are just getting started, though, and I wanted to create a detailed blueprint for new financial planners that would serve as a better introduction to the profession. It's a resource for the next generation of financial planners seeking to work alongside the soon-to-be-retiring founder generation and a roadmap that will guide aspiring financial planners in their pursuit to assume leadership of the profession. If I can provide that, clients will be better served, and the knowledge transfer between new planners and aging founders will be smooth and successful, helping the profession flourish.

In the chapters to come, I will walk you through exactly what you need to do to find success as a financial planner. Our profession needs you, and we are so very glad to have you.

CHAPTER 1

— • —

A COMPELLING CAREER

"*My job is to awaken possibility in other people.*"
—Benjamin Zander

When the financial planner came on the scene fifty years ago, they mainly conducted financial transactions for families or clients. That's not the case today. The profession has evolved, and financial planners have become an integral part of the family unit they serve.

You might say the financial planner is the "Family CFO." They help with all aspects of a client's financial life, including, but not limited to, investments, insurance, estate, tax, retirement, debt, credit, budgeting, and business planning. Other areas financial planners assist clients with could include:

- Buying and selling primary and secondary residences

- Other real estate and land transactions

- Equity compensation (stock options) maximization strategies

- College funding

- Financial literacy and education training for the client's children

- Charitable giving/Legacy planning

- Career coaching

- Employee benefits planning

- Eldercare/End of life planning

Financial planners are also available as a sounding board for clients who are thinking about making any type of decision. Since they are the client's trusted advisor, they often find themselves helping clients through emotional times, especially if one of the four D's is involved: Death, Disability, Depression, or Drugs. Over your career, you will encounter at least one of the four D's at some point. It's part of the relational nature of the profession.

The daily role of a financial planner is much more than picking stocks and making trades as it was decades ago. It has a unique relational aspect, like law, medicine, accounting and other service professions; as the profession has matured and is more widely viewed like other established service professions, having a relationship with a financial planner is more common.

Financial planners have expanded the scope of their services to help clients in all aspects of life. They operate as the "quarterback" of the client's financial situation, sometimes bringing in additional experts such as realtors, bankers, accountants, attorneys, and insurance specialists when it serves the client's needs. This unique role and knowledge of client affairs position the financial planner to have life-changing impacts on the clients they serve.

Here are the most cited reasons why people choose a career in financial planning over other well-established professions:

Rewarding career — The work you will do for your clients as a financial planner is very fulfilling because of the long-term relationships you develop with the families you serve. You can see the fruits of your labor firsthand by watching your client's stress and anxiety melt away, even when their plan needs work, and they must make some hard decisions. But they have newfound confidence with a competent financial planner guiding them. You also assist them with financial and life decisions and realize they look to you to guide them through life successfully. That is a lot of responsibility that should not be taken lightly. But it should also excite you!

Flexible — Even if you are an employee working as part of a larger team, as long as you are available to meet with your clients, usually 8 a.m. to 5 p.m. during the workday, most of the work in financial planning can be done anywhere. If/when you become a business owner, you will have even more control over your schedule as your role shifts to focus on bringing in clients and managing the firm.

Remember, the more business development centric the position is, the more flexibility you have for being out of the office prospecting and meeting people.

Intellectually stimulating — To become a successful financial planner, you must possess deep knowledge in many technical areas that your clients will encounter throughout different stages of their life. Financial planning is not a profession where you can easily become a subject matter expert and coast for the rest of your career. So, if you are a lifelong learner, this career is a great match for you.

Income potential — This depends greatly on the business model you choose to start your career and your current skill set. But starting in an entry-level salaried position in a support role, you can expect to start around $50k–$60k/year plus bonus and benefits. As your career progresses, along with your skills and confidence, and you become the Lead Planner and primary point of contact for client relationships, you can easily work into the low six figures.

From that point on, the ability to bring in clients and directly generate revenue is the most scalable way to increase your income. Remember, your income is not capped. Established planners can earn mid-six to seven figures depending on the value they bring to their clients and organizations.

Shape the profession — Since financial planning is still relatively new and evolving, the next generation of planners will significantly impact its direction. In more established professions such as law, medicine, and accounting, it is difficult to innovate and move the needle. Financial planning is ripe for opportunities, such as what Michael Kitces and Alan Moore have done with XY Planning Network. If you are the type of person who wants to leave your mark on your profession, you can do that in the financial planning world.

Does this sound great, or what? For a lot of people, the answer is yes! However, you should reflect on the question, *"Is this profession right for me?"* Let's explore some typical characteristics of financial planners so you may compare these skill sets with your interests and passions to ensure this is a path for you to consider.

What personality types thrive in the financial planning world? You can succeed as an introvert or extrovert. Some more analytical financial planners love math, numbers, and spreadsheets. But these are turn-offs for others. So, you want to be careful with stereotypes and overgeneralizations, but the best financial planners have a unique combination of left and right brain activities. Think of the left brain as the analytical part and the right brain as the creative part.

Can you handle learning all the financial concepts and topics? To be a successful planner, you must master a substantial amount of information that can frequently change (think tax law changes, etc.), but will at least change periodically. That might scare off the extrovert who loves to develop relationships, but it shouldn't. The profession has a major shortage of client-facing types where your primary responsibility is managing the client relationship. Currently, there's no shortage of analytical types. This creates an enormous opportunity for anyone seeking a client-facing role.

What firms have learned is that since people who possess equal preferences in both the left and right brain activities are rare, they try to hire one person in an advisor role who is more client relationship-focused and another who is more analytical-focused financial planner to work on the client situations together. This doesn't mean you cannot succeed with clients if you are analytical or introverted. Many firm owners and entrepreneurs who are the most successful and highest-earning planners I know are introverts. It is okay to be an introvert, and you can have lots of success in this profession!

Also, it is worth noting that the difference between introvert and extrovert is that introvert wants to be alone to recharge their batteries after being around people all day. It doesn't mean they are less effective or confident when dealing with people.

Generally, you can succeed if you have these qualities already and/or want to attain them:

- Enjoy helping others and seeing them succeed

- Well above average natural curiosity

- Problem-solving mindset

- Ability to read people

- Can thrive under pressure, high stress, unstructured environment

- Well above average listening, empathy, sympathy ability

- Think quickly on your feet

- Takes charge and shows initiative

Day in The Life of a Financial Planner

"I am so grateful I am a financial planner. I get to come to work everyday to help my clients have a better life. I couldn't imagine doing anything else."

—Megan W.

In case you are wondering how a financial planner spends their time, here are some details as to how a financial planner can spend their day.

Daily activities include keeping up with news and current events, meeting with clients via phone, video, and in-person, analyzing client data to formulate recommendations, researching investment opportunities, tax law, and marketing for new clients.

Sample daily agendas for experienced planners:

Example 1

8:00 a.m. — Review the Wilson financial plan with Associate Planner

9:30–11:00 — Financial Plan presentation meeting with the Wilsons

11:30–12:30 p.m. — Lunch with local CPA

1:00–2:00 — Respond to emails and phone messages

3:00–4:00 — Present webinar to local Chamber of Commerce on Business Planning Post COVID-19

5:00–6:00 p.m. — Review "to do's," reflect, write out goals to accomplish for next day

Example 2

6:30–8 a.m. — Rotary breakfast and networking meeting

9:00–11:00 — Strategy session for upcoming Discovery meeting with the Browns

11:30–1:30 p.m. — Lunch with team

2:00–3:00 — Phone call with the Smiths to discuss lake house purchase

3:00–5:30 — Catch up on outstanding client tasks, emails, and voicemails

5:30–6:00 p.m. — Reflect and prepare for following day

Example 3

9:30–12:00 p.m. — Continuing education meeting on SECURE ACT

12:30–2:00 — Lunch with spouse

2:30–4:30 — Modeling scenarios for upcoming Plan Presentation meeting with the Johnsons

5:30–6:30 p.m. — Initial prospect meeting with the Jacksons

Example 4

9:00 a.m. — Team meeting

10:00 — Video call with prospective client

11:00–12:00 p.m. — Rebalance AAA client's investment accounts

1:00–3:00 — Research tax question from the Greens and develop a response

4:00–5:30 — Record bio and value proposition videos for updated website

7:00–9:00 p.m. — Attend current client's open house for new business grand opening

Sample daily agendas for New Planners

Note: Here are some examples of what a day in the life of a new planner could look like. Notice there is less time spent on business development and advice delivery and more on the preparation, follow-up, and support functions.

Example 1

7:30 a.m. — Prepare prospect materials for the Smith family prospect meeting

8:00–9:30 — Attend Smith family prospect meeting

10:00–10:30 — Debrief with Senior Planner on Smith meeting

10:30–11:00 — Prepare the Smith family's prospect meeting follow-up notes

11:30–12:30 p.m. — Lunch

1:00–2:00 — Respond to emails and phone messages

2:00–4:00 — Prepare retirement scenarios for upcoming Jones family Brainstorming Meeting

4:00–6:00 p.m. — Review the Johnson family employee benefits options and call to walk them through selections for open enrollment

Example 2

8:30–9:00 a.m. — Morning reading, email, and voicemail check

9:30–11:30 — Follow-up on prior day's and overnight client service requests

11:30–12:00 p.m. — Lunch

12:30–1:30 — Meet with Senior Planner to review Jones retirement scenarios

1:30–2:00 — Send the Brown family a distribution from brokerage account to cover quarterly tax payment

2:30–4:30 — Attend Jones Brainstorming meeting and present various retirement options

5–6:00 p.m. — Debrief with Senior Planner on Jones Brainstorming meeting

Example 3:

8:00–9:00 a.m. — Attend a webinar on tax planning for high-income clients

9:00–9:30 — Phone call with the Andersons to discuss long-term care insurance

10:00–10:30 — Prepare for Data Gathering meeting with the Price family

11:00–12:30 p.m. — Lead Data Gathering meeting with the Prices

1:00–2:00 — Lunch

2:30–3:00 — Debrief with Senior Planner on Price Data Gathering meeting

3:30–5:30 — Input Price data into software systems and begin building a financial plan

6:00 p.m. — Review outstanding items and develop a priority list for tomorrow

Example 4:

7:00–8:00 a.m. — Meet with interns, create priority list and delegate if necessary

8:00–9:00 — Research and prepare an email for the Senior Planner to review for the Green family question on the best way to give funds to their alma mater

9:00–11:00 — Update financial plan for the Peterson family Updated Financial Plan meeting next week

1:00–1:00 p.m. — Attend FPA (Financial Planning Association) Chapter Meeting/Nexgen lunch CE presentation on Estate Planning Strategies for Small Business Owners

1:00–2:00 — Return phone calls

2:00–3:00 — Call financial planning software vendor to discuss the best way to model closely held business sale

3:00–4:00 — Phone call with Mrs. Jackson about her question on her statement

4:00–5:00 — Call client account custodian to check the status of a trade, money movement, and address change on Mr. Richardson's account

5:00–6:00 p.m. — Review and prepare for the following day.

These agendas can vary, and you should expect some long days when starting because there is so much to learn. But they should give you an idea of how you will spend your time as a professional financial planner. I would also encourage you to review these activities and reflect on what you think you would enjoy the most so you can begin laying the framework for your ideal position.

Key Takeaways

- Financial planning is still newer than most professions where you can affect change.

- You are more than the "stock picker" or "financial person."

- Your daily schedule can vary depending on the stage of your career.

- There is a place and path to success for all personality types in financial planning.

- There is a huge demand for financial planning services.

Action Steps

- Review Chapter 1 Materials using this QR Code.

- Write down the top three skills you think you possess.

- Write down five things that you enjoy doing.

- Ask yourself the following questions:

  ○ Do I have the characteristics commonly associated with a career as a financial planner as laid out in Chapter 1?

  ○ If not, what skills do I need to develop further?

  ○ If yes, how much satisfaction do I derive from helping people? 1-10? Hint: if a five or more—consider financial planning!

CHAPTER 2

—·—

CHOOSING YOUR CAREER PATH

"The only way to do great work is to love what you do. If you haven't found it yet, keep looking. Don't settle."
—Steve Jobs

What is your first step to becoming a financial planner?

First, you must understand all the various business models available and the main career entry points before taking the next step in your journey. One of the differentiating attributes of the financial planning profession is that you can enter the business in many ways, which can be a bit confusing. However, it gives you great flexibility in how you want your career to look.

Once you understand the pathways to entry, you will know what education, licenses, and training you will need because all firms and career opportunities are different!

Here are the main career entry point channels for new planners with the expected minimum licensing requirements, plus a few examples of the different companies in each channel:

There are six main channels through which aspiring financial planners can enter the business. Scan the QR code for a more detailed comparison of the channels.

Also, be sure to check out the 12 Tribes of Financial Planning Career Resource visual developed by Luke Dean, PhD, Nathan Harness, PhD, and Craig Lemoine, PhD.

Channel-Specific Activities

Let's explore specific daily activities you will likely spend time doing in each channel.

Insurance

Since you are being hired as an agent for the insurance company, the company will expect you to begin generating revenue within a few weeks to a few months. Hiring and training new agents can be costly. Because insurance companies generate most of their profit from selling insurance products, they expect you to generate commissions to cover the initial cost of licensing and training you.

You will most likely be paid as a 1099 contractor instead of a W-2 (see Chapter 2 Materials for details on differences between 1099 and W2 classifications) employee because you are responsible for your materials, setting your schedule, and generating revenue on your own. However, you could also be classified as a statutory employee since there is a carve-out in the tax code for insurance companies. This means you will be taxed like a 1099 contractor but receive a W2. Insurance companies sometimes set it up this way so their agents can access group benefits such as health and pension plans. Expect to spend most of your day prospecting for new clients to offer your products and services.

The emphasis will be on products, though, and you will go through significant formal sales training in this channel. Prospecting can take many forms but means reaching out to people you know or do not know to try and get them to agree to a meeting with you so you can try and sell one of your company's products. Insurance companies typically have all of their new hires create a "200 list," which is a list of 200 people you know—usually family and friends for you to start contacting to arrange appointments. Your success in this model is based on specific targets for your activity, such as you calling 100 people per day, talking to ten of them, making three scheduled appointments, and you make one sale.

Also, since insurance companies were built around the commissioned-based compensation structure, there is typically no guaranteed or base salary when you join. At least when starting, you will keep a percentage ranging from 25–60% of the commissions you generate. Usually, there is no base salary, but most insurance companies offer a draw. A draw is a pay structure in which the company fronts you with a small monthly stipend, which will be repaid later after you begin generating commission income when you get up and going. A draw is, in effect, a short-term loan paid to you as a salary and recouped by the company when you generate revenue from fees or commissions.

This is an up or out position, meaning you will be terminated if you are not able to generate the minimum commission amount per year, which differs among firms but usually is $50,000 per year minimum, so you will need to be able to generate at least $50,000 worth of commissions your first year. So you have a reference point; annuities can pay commissions of 6% of the total annuity amount, permanent life insurance such as universal life (UL), variable universal life (VUL), and whole life (WL) can pay a commission of 100% of the first year's premium for the policy. And these production goals will increase each year, usually for the first three years; for example, in year 2, you may be expected to generate $75k; in year 3, $100k, and so forth.

Wirehouse

Similar to the insurance channel in that, unless you join a team where a senior advisor pays you a salary, the company will expect you to begin making sales to generate commissions from investment products (mutual funds, managed money, etc.) primarily. There might be some insurance products, but this will be an investment product sales-heavy position. They may have an office, all of your technology like software and phone systems, and administrative help in place for you. Still, once you complete their training program, you will be responsible for generating revenue.

After learning about the company and its products and services, expect to spend most of your day "prospecting." You will go through significant formal sales training in this channel. There might be some guaranteed base compensation, probably structured as a draw. These positions are an 'up or out' situation for new hires too, meaning you must meet the production goals: typically, at least $10 million in net new assets under management per year for the first few years, or they will likely terminate you. If you can find a position on an existing team, these production goals will be spread across the team, not you individually, which can help you get over the hump. The wirehouses have some of the most thorough training programs in the profession. Some can be as long as three years, exposing you to a depth of product knowledge and sales tactics.

Asset Management

These are larger companies that got their start by emphasizing the investment management side of the business. Many asset management companies provide de minimis retirement planning, while others offer full-service, "private client" offerings that mirror an RIA firm's comprehensive financial planning services.

You can expect significant formal sales and product training in this channel, primarily due to the size of the organizations. Entry-level hires start taking inbound calls from the firm's customers who have questions about their accounts. Then, as your career progresses, you can move into more of an ongoing advisory relationship with a certain number of clients. One item worth noting here is that it is not uncommon for these firms to assign 400–500 or more clients to one advisor. In comparison, a typical financial planner in an RIA might be working with 150–200 clients at the most. If you are not able to successfully pass your licensing exams by the second try, you will likely be terminated.

Fee-Based RIA

These firms utilize a broker-dealer affiliation for transactional (brokerage) accounts. They receive a commission, and they also have an RIA relationship for advisory accounts, where they receive a fee and are sometimes referred to as dually registered or hybrid RIAs. Dually registered means they must register with the Financial Industry Regulatory Authority (FINRA) and the Securities Exchange Commission (SEC).

They tend to be independent and smaller in size. For example, a sole proprietor with a few million in assets under management all the way up to "mega" RIAs with 600+ employees and $200+ billion in assets. These firms usually focus more on the full financial planning offering, but some focus primarily on managing client investments and not so much on the planning aspect. You'll find that many of these firms are founded by other financial planners who left the insurance, brokerage, and wirehouse channels seeking the autonomy to serve their clients without having to answer to a larger company dictating guidelines and requiring quotas.

Entry-level planner hires can start as an Associate Planner (sitting 2nd chair) role where you would spend most of your time supporting more experienced planners (1st chair) to serve their clients, doing anything you can to free your senior planners up, including administrative, client service, and operational work. These positions are W2 salaried positions usually. You also can earn incentive bonuses from new clients, assets, and revenue growth.

Fee-Only RIA

The Fee-Only RIA firms resemble fee-based RIAs, except they have no affiliation with a broker-dealer and do not receive commissions because there are no product sales associated with this model. These firms usually emphasize financial planning and investment management for a fee paid directly by the client. Since they are 100% independent, they can provide their services to clients however they see fit. In this channel, firms keep all the revenue they generate but must pay all the expenses providing a great deal of autonomy.

Suppose an RIA hires you, and you are licensed to give investment advice. In that case, you are registered as an IAR (Investment

Advisor Representative), which usually means you have passed the NASAA (North American Securities Administrators Association) Series 65 exam and/or are a CERTIFIED FINANCIAL PLAN-NER™ (CFP®), Chartered Financial Analyst (CFA), Charter Financial Consultant (ChFC), Personal Financial Specialist (PFS) or Chartered Investment Counselor (CIC). It is a good policy to check with your state for the requirements to become an IAR.

Most of these firms will hire new planners as W2 employees. Depending on the firm's size, be prepared for a limited amount of formal training and lots of on-the-job training. It is not uncommon for new hires to be involved in client meetings from the beginning since they are in a support position, and these firms need you to get up to speed in working with clients very quickly without a lot of formal structured training.

Bank/Credit Union

"I would encourage anyone looking to get started to not worry too much about finding the perfect channel of entry right off the bat. Educate yourself on what is out there and available, but get started wherever you can, then you can always move to a different channel as your career progresses."

—Peg M., started in the insurance channel and moved to a wirehouse

Banks are closest to the Wirehouse model. How? They're large financial institutions with tremendous infrastructure and large workforces. One of the benefits of joining a bank is that they already have customers you can begin targeting for financial planning, wealth management, or Bank Trust-type services. New hires in the bank structure are W2 employees and will be tasked with converting traditional banking clients over to more profitable investment management and financial planning services. The core set of solutions centers around what banks do best; Certificates of Deposit (CDs), mortgages, annuities, checking & savings accounts, managed money, mutual funds, etc.

Many employee credit unions want to be able to offer financial planning to their clients. If you take this route, you could end up in a credit union branch inside an employer (a large company like Walmart, John Deere, Raytheon, etc.) facility. You would be tasked with securing walk-in business from the workers/employees visiting the branch for other banking business.

Remember, foot traffic in banks is not what it used to be, thanks to online banking. Another challenge with this model is trying to convince someone who has always had all their money in CDs to go through a planning process and diversify their portfolio or persuading a client who only owns an insurance policy to do financial planning. But if you can consistently convince people like this, you will succeed with this model and the others.

Here is a chart to help you compare the key traits of each channel.

	Insurance	Wirehouse	Asset Mgmt	Fee-Only Registered Investment Advisor	Fee-Based Registered Investment Advisor	Bank/Credit Union
Autonomy From Parent Company	Low	Low	Low	High	Med–High	Low
Product/Service offering	Med–High	Med–High	Med–High	Med–High	Med–High	Med
Formal Training	High	High	High	Low	Low–Med	Med–High
Marketing Support	High	High	High	Low	Low	Med
Compliance Burden	High	High	High	Low–Med	High	High

It is possible to join a team of existing professionals in the insurance and wirehouse models where you would not be in production (meaning you would not be required to start selling right away). Instead, you would support the "producers," who are usually more experienced and responsible for generating revenue via new clients.

These positions are becoming more popular as the profession fights to attract talent. However, remember that even if you accept one of these positions, the company will want you to become a full-fledged producer, usually within a few years, to recoup their investment in training and taking the risk of hiring you.

A Financial Planner's Three Main Career Paths

There are three main career paths for a financial planner once inside your channel. Each one of these channels provides you with its own set of options about how you want your career to look.

Entrepreneur Career Path - You start your business underneath any of the above channels and are responsible for building your business and generating enough revenue to support yourself.

Employee Career Path - You join an existing firm and receive a salary your employer pays to service their clients and help them build their businesses. The key takeaway is that you are working for someone else and relying on them to bring in clients and generate revenue.

Hybrid Career Path - This path combines employee and entrepreneur paths in that you join an existing business and receive a salary from working with another planner's clients. Still, you also have the flexibility to bring in your clients and start building your business part-time.

Personality and Workstyle Preference Tools

It might be challenging to discover which career path fits you best. If this is you, don't stress about it. It takes some people many years to find their true passions, skills, and desires.

Here are some tools that can help you determine where you might be the best fit.

Kolbe A™ Index - This assessment provides excellent insight into how you prefer to do things, known as Conation. It measures your preferred action method in four modes: *Fact Finder, Follow Thru, Quickstart,* and *Implementer.*

For example, do you lead by asking many questions and gathering data? Or do you start brainstorming ideas? Do you start designing systems and thinking of structure and processes? Or do you start by building a tangible prototype, drawing pictures, and making models? This measures the Conative part of your mind and is not a personality assessment.

The Quickstarts have new ideas all the time and embrace chaos and change. They're naturally wired to view taking risks and failure differently and can be good candidates for starting their firms immediately. Fact Finders seek lots of information before deciding. Follow Thrus are structured, process, and organizational people who do well in organizations that mobilize Quickstart's ideas. This assessment takes about 15 minutes to complete and costs about $50.

For further information, visit https://www.kolbe.com

DISC- This assessment measures the Affective (feeling) part of your mind. It provides

insight and/or confirmation on whether you are wired more like an extrovert or introvert.

DISC stands for **D**ominance **I**nfluence **S**teadiness **C**ompliance. The D's are the type–A entrepreneurial type who takes risks and starts businesses from scratch. Influencers are outgoing and social and excel in client-facing roles in financial planning firms. People higher in the S category are your natural service and support people who thrive in task-based roles and are steady worker bee types.

High C's tend to be in more research, analytical, and non-client-facing positions within firms. This assessment takes about 30 minutes and costs about $50.

For further information, visit https://www.paragonresources.com

__Strengthsfinder__ - Like the DISC assessment, Strengthsfinder measures the Affective part of the mind like a traditional personality test. The results are built around a set of 34 themes which are ranked in order based on your responses to the questions. The results are then categorized into four main quadrants: Strategic Thinking, Relationship Building, Influencing, and Executing.

You receive a detailed breakdown of your top ten themes. Here are some examples: Learner, Harmony, Activator, Consistency, and Communication. The analysis is very detailed and can be quite helpful in uncovering and/or confirming your preferred methods. They don't set out to "fix you" as some providers do. Instead, the results make you hyper-aware of your traits and how to use them to further your success. This assessment takes about 30 minutes and costs about $50.

For further information, visit www.gallup.com/cliftonstrengths/en/home.aspx

__Myers-Briggs__- Originally developed to assist college students in selecting a study path, this assessment is now the most recognized personality profile around the world. It helps you to identify your natural preferences in four areas of personality: how you direct and receive energy, how you take in information, how you decide and come to conclusions, and how you approach the outside world.

Based on your responses, it classifies you as one of 16 personality types. (E) Extraversion or (I) Introversion, (S) Sensing or (N) Intuition, (T) Thinking or (F) Feeling, (J) Judging or (P) Perceiving. The assessment takes 10–20 minutes and costs about $50.

For further information, visit https://www.myersbriggs.org

__Enneagram__- This personality assessment has gained momentum in the last few years. The structure includes a set of nine distinct personality types, each number indicating a personality type. The nine types are The Reformer, The Helper, The Achiever, The Individualist, The Investigator, The Loyalist, The Enthusiast, The Challenger, and The Peacemaker. The report provides a detailed description of what types of stressors and motivators for your personality type. The assessment takes about 10 minutes and is about $12.

Source: https://www.enneagraminstitute.com/type-descriptions/

If you have the means, you can obtain a large amount of data about yourself and how you are likely to operate at your highest and best use to succeed professionally and personally. I would suggest investing some time and money on the front end to gain ultimate clarity into your **Who** are you, **Why** you are doing this, and **How** are you going to do it? It's a good practice for career seekers to include their results (top 5 strengths, Kolbe A index, etc.) on their resume and LinkedIn profile to show potential employers they have put forth above-average effort and financial outlay to invest in their career by learning more about themselves.

Another good way to learn more about the various channels of the financial planning profession is to reach out to planners in your local area or network. Tell them you are researching various business models in the profession and ask them if you can spend 20 to 30 minutes interviewing them to assist with the research you are compiling.

Most financial planners in the profession want to pay it forward and help aspiring planners and are generally open to spending a few minutes with you. This is also an excellent way to establish good professional relationships as you look to get your foot in the door. Developing relationships as you search for a job, will provide you with better results than cold-calling places and asking for a job directly.

Key Takeaways

- Familiarize yourself with the challenges and benefits of the six main channels of entry:

  - Wirehouse

  - Insurance Company

  - Asset Management Firm

  - Fee-only Registered Investment Advisor

  - Fee-Based Registered Investment Advisor

  - Bank/Credit Union

- Review daily activities and position structure to envision where you might fit the best.

- Consider investing time and resources into personality assessments and profiles to better understand who you are and where you fit in the profession.

Action Items

- Review Chapter 2 Materials using this QR Code.

- Add your results of the personality, career, and work style assessments to your resume.

- Reach out to at least three firms in your area to learn about their business model.

- Ask yourself the following questions:

  - Which channel do I think I would have the best chance for success when starting in my career?

CHAPTER 3

—.—

HOW TO PROPERLY VET POTENTIAL EMPLOYERS

"We are surrounded by data, but starved for insights"
—Jay Baer

Now that you know the career entry points and career paths and have a better understanding of what a financial planner does, and how you might fit in within the profession, we will explore how to screen for the hiring firms that are the best fit for you.

Finding The Best Firm to Work For

The financial planning profession is riddled with jargon and complexities that make it difficult to understand the differences between firms. Understanding the entire anatomy of a financial planning firm is essential to finding the right firm for you, and compensation is a component of getting the complete picture.

How Do Financial Planning Firms Get Paid?

In the profession, although there are many ways a firm can generate revenue, there are two primary ways firms accept compensation:

- *Commission* — Commissions are payments made by a company to a financial professional upon the sale of a financial product. The types of financial products can range from insurance to mutual funds to annuities. Under this basis of compensation, everything is tied to production. No sales = No income.

- *Fee-For-Service* — A fee-for-service is a payment made by a consumer/client to a financial advisory firm in exchange for a service. This is how professionals in other industries are compensated. This type of arrangement can be made in several ways:

1. **Hourly Rate** — Firms are paid a flat hourly rate in exchange for time spent doing financial analysis and meeting with clients.

2. **Fixed Retainer Fee** — Firms are paid an ongoing fixed fee for a set level of advisor services, which could include investment management, financial planning, and access as needed to the planner, without a change in fees paid.

   a. This could be set as an annual retainer established at the beginning of each year based on how much time the firm thinks it will take to serve the client.

   b. Some firms charge a subscription fee which is structured similarly to a monthly Netflix, gym membership, Spotify subscription, etc.

3. **Assets Under Management (AUM)** — This compensation model is based on assets a financial planning firm is investing for clients and will vary based on market performance, savings rates, or withdrawals. Currently, this is the most common type of fee structure, but retainers and subscriptions are

becoming more popular.

From these different avenues of compensation, three primary distinctions are used to define how firms receive revenue. While the exact definition varies across various organizations, like the Certified Financial Planner Board of Standards (CFP Board), Financial Planning Association (FPA), and National Association of Personal Financial Advisors (NAPFA), firms can be categorized as *Commission-Only, Fee-Based, or Fee-Only.*

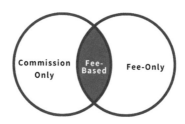

A ***Commission-Only*** firm does not receive any fees directly from clients. All revenue the firm generates is from companies in exchange for selling a financial product to a client.

A ***Fee-Based*** firm accepts both commissions and fees-for-service. These activities can be independent of one another. For example, some clients will either be on commission or fee-for-service. And some clients will experience an overlap where a firm receives both a commission and a fee from a client for the services rendered. In evaluating a fee-based firm, it's good to ask questions to determine where the firm lies on the spectrum. Are they doing more commission or fee-for-service work?

A ***Fee-Only*** firm accepts compensation solely from fees paid by clients. There are no commissions earned, referral fees, kickbacks, or compensation other than what is received directly from the client.

Why Does it Matter?

Conversations around industry compensation models focus on consumer awareness and needs. As a job seeker, use the elements of a compensation model as a litmus test to gain insight into the firm's approach, focus, and culture.

The compensation model can give insight into the types of relationships a firm cultivates with its clients. A firm that is more commission-driven tends to be transactional with a propensity for sales. They often work with more clients with broader needs and means.

Conversely, a fee-only firm tends to have a more relationship-based approach to clients, lending itself to working with a smaller number of clients more personally.

The popular adage, "You get what you pay for," holds throughout financial services. Are you seeking a firm focused on investments, insurance, or financial planning? How a firm gets paid determines its focus. Firms receiving all revenue from commissions tend to have extensive expertise in a specific area. For example, those selling insurance are probably more focused on insurance than other financial areas. Fee-only firms tend to be more comprehensive financial planning or investment management focused since clients pay a fee for their expertise across all areas.

One of the buzzwords common in the financial planning industry has been "conflicts of interest." Firms have been seeking ways to minimize their perceived conflicts of interest with clients. While each compensation model has inherent flaws, the industry has been trending towards the fee-only model, where advisors take a fiduciary responsibility to always act in a client's best interest.

Proponents of the fee-only model feel accepting commissions can incentivize an advisor to make recommendations to clients based on the additional compensation they stand to receive. Here is an example of a potential conflict a commission-only advisor could face.

Sal, the advisor for the Smith family, only needs to sell one more annuity to be eligible for the Top 50 Club with his company ABC Financial. Each year ABC Financial takes the top 50 advisors, based on commissions generated, on an all-expense paid two-week European cruise. Sal has always wanted to take his family to Europe; they love cruising and going on trips. One of Sal's clients, the Smith family, inherited $100,000 and wants to meet with Sal to determine the best place to put their money. The Smiths mentioned to Sal they would like to use the inherited funds to upgrade their kitchen, master bathroom, and shore up their emergency fund savings. Sal recommends that they put the funds into a new annuity to go along with the three other annuities the Smiths already have as part of their plan. Now Sal is qualified to go on the cruise.

Fee-based advisors often have solid reasons for selecting a given model, such as client demand, an increased rate of client implementation, and providing a concierge service model for financial products their clients need. Look for these firms to have internal controls to disclose and manage potential conflicts of interest.

Fee-only advisors feel their model is the most transparent since the compensation comes directly from the client. However, they still have conflicts of interest. Here is an example of a potential conflict a fee-only advisor could face.

Mary is a fee-only advisor who does financial planning and manages the Peterson's portfolio, which is currently $1 million. Mary charges the Petersons 1% of the portfolio or $10,000 annually to provide these services. The Petersons recently sold a piece of land for $500,000, and they met with Mary to discuss *what to do with the new funds. Jim Peterson would like to give $250,000 to the University of Florida, and Sally Peterson would like to provide $250,000 to the University of Georgia. After hearing what the Petersons would like to do, Mary tells them they should not gift the funds to their alma maters but instead transfer them into the portfolio she manages for them. Hence, the fee she charges them on their portfolio increases to $15,000 annually.*

It is virtually impossible to eliminate all conflicts of interest, so be aware of how they might occur. This is also why it is so refreshing to hear business people state verbally when they have a conflict versus not addressing and trying to bury it in the various written disclosures that must be provided based on regulatory requirements.

Which one is right for me?

Your philosophies should drive your decision to join a firm and buy into its compensation model. There is no right or wrong answer. The choice is different for everyone and is another reason to ensure you are clear on the other compensation structures so you can form your own opinions.

The compensation model should not be a blind qualifier or disqualifier of a firm. Use the terms fee-only and fee-based as intended, as a uniform educator and high-level explanation vehicle. It is not a replacement for the questions job seekers should ask to understand the actual sources and amounts of compensation earned. Discover what is important to you and what aligns with your personal, cultural, and business values—and find a firm that matches. Also, remember that you do not want to use the terms fee-only and fee-based incorrectly. For example, if you are interviewing with a fee-only firm and refer to them as fee-based, you will probably not be invited back for another interview. There are some strong opinions, and people on both sides are easily offended if you refer to their compensation model incorrectly.

Forms Overview

In this section, I want to give you an overview of the different forms you'll need to familiarize yourself with. They are the Advisor Disclosure Vet (ADV) Parts 1, 2, and 3, SEC IAPD (Investment Advisor Public Disclosure), Financial Industry Regulatory Authority (FINRA) Broker check, and Verify a CFP® Professional.

Other than reviewing the firm's website, another way to find detailed information about a firm is to use the available governmental resources. Form ADV is a form that the SEC requires Registered Investment Advisor (RIA) firms to file annually, describing all areas of their business operations in detail. It can be found here: https://adviserinfo.sec.gov.

If used correctly, this can be a treasure trove of information for job seekers. When researching companies, here are some areas to pay attention to better understand the firm. These areas of note can give you a better idea of what questions to ask when you go in for your interview:

- Item 1 Section F lists the business address, contact information, and hours of operation.

- Item 2 Section A tells you whether they are a large RIA, meaning they typically manage over 100 million in assets.

- Item 3 Section A states how the company is organized: LLC, Corporation, Partnership, etc.

- Item 5 Section A lists how many employees work at the firm.

- Item 5 Section D tells you all about their client makeup,

including their number of clients, if they are high net worth, and exact totals on assets under management.

- Item 5 Section E describes how they are compensated. If a firm you are interviewing with says they are fee-only, and the "*commission*" box under this section is checked, you ask a few clarifying questions during your interview.

- Item 5 Section G lists what services the firm provides. If the "*financial planning*" box is not checked and the firm says they do financial planning, you need to ask clarifying questions during your interview.

- Item 5 Section H spells out how many clients the firm did financial planning for. This is important if you seek a firm focusing on financial planning. For example, if you notice in Section D that the firm has 500 clients, but in Section H, "0" is selected, you need to follow up on the discrepancy. It could have been an error *you* found, making you very valuable to the firm and you haven't even been hired yet!

- Section 5.K lists all of the custodians or companies that hold the client's assets that the firm manages.

- Item 6 lists other business activities; sometimes you might see #6 Insurance broker or agent, #12 Accountant or Accounting Firm, and #13 Lawyer or Law Firm selected, but this will tell you about other affiliations the firm has.

- Schedule A lists all the owners of the firm. This is important because some firms might say in an interview that there are multiple owners, and you could be an owner someday too. It is always good to check here to ensure that the other owners are indeed listed.

Part 2 of the ADV is a special brochure the firm must provide to clients and prospective clients each year that lists their activities in "plain English." It is best practice to study the entire document, but here are some sections to focus on:

- Item 2 Lists any material changes.

- Item 4 is a description of the firm. Ensure this matches what they say in the interviews and what is listed on the website.

- Item 5 shows the fee Schedule. You want to ensure the fees are reasonable. E.g., the industry standard for asset management is 1% up to $1 million in portfolio value, .75% for $1–2 million, .50% for $2–3 million, and .25% for $3 million +. There are hundreds of fee schedules, but this should give you an idea for comparison. Also, some firms do not charge separately for financial planning while others do, and those fees can range anywhere from $250 per plan up to $25,000 or more for an initial comprehensive plan.

- Item 8 discusses the Investment management philosophy of the firm. This is important to review if you prefer active investing (you think the market can be outperformed consistently) over passive (you think the market is mostly efficient and cannot be outperformed consistently) investing. You should have a solid understanding of each and where you stand on how to invest client money. You should strive to join a firm with which you share similar beliefs.

- Item 11 spells out the firm's Code of Ethics. Read through thoroughly to ensure they align with yours.

Form ADV Part 3, Client Relationship Summary (CRS), is another form required by the SEC to further assist prospective clients in understanding their relationship with a Registered Investment Advisor or a Broker Dealer. It has 5 sections:

Section 1 - Introduction to the Firm

Section 2 - Relationships and Services

Section 3 - Fees, Costs, Conflicts and Standard of Contact

Section 4 - Disciplinary History

Section 5 - Additional Information

I have included a sample of a full ADV report in the Chapter 3 Materials. Keep in mind that the ADV provides information on the firm. Suppose the firm you are considering is not an independent RIA. In that case, the ADV will not be as helpful because it represents the entire organization, not the specific advisor you may be interviewing with. For example, if you pull the ADV for a wirehouse such as UBS, it will provide information summarizing the 5,000 + financial professionals it employs. This is why it is also very beneficial for you to check out each of the firm owners or members of the firm you will be interviewing with.

"These tools were immensely helpful to me while narrowing down which firms I wanted to interview with."

—Ryan Grava, CFP Program student and aspiring financial planner

Here are some resources for you to look further into people with whom you might be working:

FINRA Brokercheck — https://brokercheck.finra.org/

This will provide you with confirmation on the years of experience of a registered representative or anyone affiliated with a broker-dealer/FINRA registered firm, what securities exams they have passed, how many licenses they have, and if they have any client disclosures. If there is a client disclosure, there will be a summary provided, and depending on the circumstances might be something you want to bring up in an interview.

Use caution; though most firms will be ecstatic you have taken this much effort to check out a potential employer, some firms with some disclosures might get defensive if you don't approach it correctly.

Ideally, you would uncover any disclosures before your first interview. Here is a sample script that you need to try and work in during the natural flow of the interview or, even better, when they ask you if you have any questions, which a good interviewer will do.

'Yes, during my research on your firm and preparation for this interview, I noticed that [insert name] had a client disclosure on their broker check. Can you tell me more about that?'

Here is a sample script if you find it after your first interview:

Hi [Insert name],

Thank you so much for interviewing me on Tuesday. It was great meeting you, seeing the office, and meeting the team. I appreciate you taking the time to speak with me about the opportunity at your firm. I was doing some research in preparation for our following interview. I noticed a few disclosures on your IAPD and/or Brokercheck. Can you tell me more about those?

Remember, too, just because there is a disclosure doesn't necessarily mean the planner you are interviewing is at fault. There is often more to the story than is included in the reports that are publicly accessible.

Investment Adviser Public Disclosure (IAPD) — https://adv iserinfo.sec.gov/

The IAPD is essentially the same thing as the Broker Check, except this is for employed Investment Advisors by RIAs who do not have a broker-dealer/FINRA-affiliated firm relationship. I have included a sample of this report in Chapter 3 materials.

CFP Board — https://www.cfp.net/verify-a-cfp-professional

This allows you to verify someone is a CERTIFIED FINANCIAL PLANNER™. It will provide the individual's current CFP® certification status, CFP Board Disciplinary History, and any Bankruptcy Disclosures in the last 10 years. I have included a sample of this report in Chapter 3, Materials. It is crucial to remember that potential employers will be performing an exhaustive search on you, starting with all social media profiles and other internet presences, then eventually references from your network and a credit, background, and potentially a drug test.

They will thoroughly research and vet you to ensure you haven't done anything that could harm their clients or their business. You should take the same care when reviewing potential employers.

How can you tell if a firm is right for you? Here are a few prompts to think through. Some of these may seem too personal and downright edgy. It's essential to approach your interviewer with humility, respect, and gratitude and ask thoughtful questions from a posture indicating that you are trying to grow in understanding. Your interviewer will appreciate the engagement and shouldn't get defensive if done correctly. Remember, you are trying to identify the ideal firm and firm structure to begin your career with. So, take it seriously.

Would you mind describing the culture of the firm for me? You want to get a sense of the culture. But realize most people you interview will say the culture is the best, especially if it is the firm owner! After all, it is their business. If you interview other team members, make sure to ask them as well.

What happens when the firm meets or exceeds goals? This is a great question that will give you additional insight into the firm's culture. You might find a wide range of answers here. For example, some firms might take their entire team to Disney World if they have a breakthrough year. Other firms might tell you, "Good job," and get you a gift card to your favorite restaurant.

Is the opening due to growth, or did someone leave? You need to approach this one carefully. Firm owners are sometimes susceptible to turnover at their firms. Ideally, your opportunity with this firm was made available because someone was promoted and/or the firm has grown so much that they need an extra planner to assist with all new clients.

How many people have held this job in the last five years? Just because there has been turnover doesn't always mean that there is something wrong with the firm or you shouldn't consider their opportunity. You need to get to the bottom of what is happening, though.

What are the most challenging aspects of the position? This question can give you insight into what you will be facing and how you need to prepare to succeed in the role. Also, it gives you a glimpse of the firm owner's expectations.

What are your expectations for me right now, one year from now, or two years? The firm should have these solidified, but if they do not, this will open a dialogue so you can get a sense of whether these expectations match your career growth goals.

Key Takeaways

- The main compensation models are Commission, Fee-Based, and Fee-Only.

- Develop and refine your philosophies around how you think financial planning should be done.

- Use the publicly available data to research everything you can about a firm you are considering.

- Don't hesitate to ask direct questions in an interview if you approach with humility, professionalism, and respect.

Action Items

- Review Chapter 3 Materials using this QR Code.

- Join the FPA and NAPFA as a student member at http s://www.financialplanningassociation.org/membership and https://www.napfa.org/membership.

- Set up an account with the CFP Board at www.cfp.net.

- Print out any of the materials you use for your research, circle and highlight the items you have questions about and pull out the documents during your interview. You want your interviewers to see how thorough and prepared you are.

CHAPTER 4

— · —

LANDING AN INTERNSHIP

"The only person you are destined to become is the person you decide to be."
—Ralph Waldo Emerson

We must all begin somewhere. And that somewhere is usually at the bottom, working our way up. Unless you were born with a trust fund, you must be willing to do the work required to get to where you envision yourself someday.

Regardless of what you might hear in the media or movies, there's no such thing as a free lunch. You must possess the humility it takes to start on the ground floor to lay the foundation for the cornerstone of a successful career. When you do, the experience of working hard and learning from others will pay off exponentially down the road. In our profession, securing an impactful internship is the first rung of the ladder.

Now that you know how to vet firms to find the best fit. Let's get you started on securing an internship or some other type of entry-level temporary employment in financial planning. This is crucial for your long-term success because it accomplishes two things:

1. It will solidify your career choice once you are exposed to an

intimate look into what financial planners do for their clients daily.

2. It will help combine all the concepts you learn in your CFP program coursework. Plus, future employers offering you permanent employment opportunities within their firms will want to see that you have completed work to demonstrate your passion for and commitment to your career.

Getting Your Resume Ready for Primetime

I have reviewed thousands of resumes. Here is how to create one that stands out and will get the attention of the hiring decision-makers.

1. First, try to avoid templates if you can, but if you need help getting started, it is an okay place to start. You could also visit your career center for specific assistance as well.

2. Keep it to one page. Recruiters and hiring managers will only spend a few seconds reviewing your resume. Since you are new/newer to your career, you shouldn't need more than one page.

3. Typical format, Name at the top just above the contact information. City, state, and zip code are acceptable. I wouldn't put your home address on a document that can be quickly circulated online. Also, include your LinkedIn profile. Then you can list your education, work experience if you have any, and software/hobbies/interests or other information section at the bottom. You can include references, but I probably wouldn't bother since references are mostly useless due to our society's hyper-litigious nature. Plus, po-

tential employers know you will only put down people who will say great things about you. If somehow they don't have all the glowing things to say, most will not share them with your new potential employer for fear of litigation/retribution if you do not get hired, and it can be traced back to the reference.

4. Include a cover letter or a summary statement at the top, just below your name. Make it easy for hiring firms to know exactly who you are, where you are located, what you want to do, and where you want to go. Don't make the decision makers work hard to try and figure out your plan. An example is *"Recent CFP Board Registered program graduate/current CFP Board Registered student seeking a paid internship position for the summer of 20XX within an RIA firm that focuses on financial planning to add value to the organization while learning the art and science of financial planning. Willing to relocate nationwide."*

5. When getting started, go ahead and include any work experience you have. Hiring firms usually prefer people that have had some type of prior office job experience.

6. When discussing your experience, strive to put the experience in tangible perspectives, such as increased sales by 12%, securing eight new customers in 2 weeks, reviewing twenty-five websites, etc.

7. Avoid talking about yourself with subjective statements like; '...hard worker, shows up on time, very organized, good with customers, strong work ethic, diligent, detail-oriented, etc.'

You want other people saying this about you and/or your experience section saying this about you. This is much more powerful than you saying it about yourself.

8. Watch your format, font, and spacing closely. You want to have a font large enough to read, suggest at least 11 pt, and don't be tempted to cram too much so it looks jumbled and causes potential employers not to want to read it.

9. Ensure you have a Word version and a PDF version. Plus, always keep a few printed copies with you to hand out.

10. Keep it updated as your coursework and career progress so you can avoid saying, "*...let me update that and send it to you...*" when you meet a potential employer.

As an aside, I think resumes are overrated because anyone can say anything about themselves, and hiring firms rarely have the time to verify everything or have the job applicant back it up. Due to this reason, they will likely become obsolete at some point in the future and probably be replaced by your LinkedIn profile because it is more dynamic and verifiable.

Here are some tips on improving your LinkedIn profile:

1. Make sure you have a LinkedIn account!

2. The professional picture is at the top.

3. Put settings as "Open to work."

4. Title—something like, "Aspiring CFP®, or CFP® student seeking an internship or full-time permanent role in a financial planning firm.

5. Summary—you can put something custom here or use the language from the summary section of your resume. It would be cool if you shot a video of yourself talking about how excited you were about your financial planning career, what financial planning means to you, and what you are looking for in a firm!

6. Experience—since it is a digital format, you can link to anything you have done professionally online. Maybe you wrote a blog post about the differences between a Traditional IRA and Roth IRA.

7. Top Skills, Publications, Specialties—you might not have any of these, which is okay. Be careful about putting something that pushes the envelope. For example, 'expert in Microsoft Excel.' If you have completed the Microsoft certification class in Excel, you can include and link to it.

8. Avoid posting personal stuff on LinkedIn. It is fine to post things about your career and internship, job search, etc., but it is a massive turnoff if you take pictures of your dog and post overly personal stuff. LinkedIn is a powerful tool that can help you in numerous ways in your career. Don't get blocked by potential employers because you post things that should go on Facebook or your other social media accounts.

Finding Opportunities and Reaching Out to Firms

"It was challenging to secure an internship, but I am glad I ended up where I did. This firm has spent a ton of time with me and has let me participate in many different activities giving me broad exposure to

all aspects of the firm. It has provided the confirmation that this is the correct career for me!"

—Mindy S., CFP program student and aspiring financial planner

Depending on your program, an internship may be required to graduate. This raises the stakes! When trying to find an internship, start by reaching out to professional associations.

Your local chapters of the Financial Planning Association (FPA —https://www.financialplanningassociation.org/) and the National Association of Personal Financial Advisors (NAPFA—www.napfa.org) know of or have members seeking interns. Some even have formal internship programs you can tap into. For example, if you are looking for a position in Denver, find the Colorado chapter of the FPA and/or the NAPFA study group and start inquiring.

Next, utilize your program professors, alums, and university career center. Your professors can help connect you with potential intern sponsors but be careful not to rely on them too much. Remember, securing an internship for you isn't their full-time job. Plus, it will be more fulfilling and develop more character if you put in the effort and take the initiative to find a great internship opportunity.

You can also check local and national job boards such as Indeed, Monster, and CareerBuilder. There probably won't be as many internship listings, but there should be some. You should also set up a job alert with the job board at the CFP Board Career Center. The CFP Board doesn't charge firms to post internship opportunities; some excellent opportunities are sometimes listed. You can also leverage your internet and search skills by finding firm websites in your target areas and reaching out directly.

With some basic investigative skills and a little time, you can find an email address for almost anyone. You want to target the decision-makers. So, the firm owners are the best place to start. Loop in any operations and/or human resources (HR) people you can also find. Smaller firms may not have HR positions due to their size.

Consider emailing or writing a letter to them directly; you can also call, but it is usually better to make a warm call versus a cold one. Keep your communication concise yet substantive. Don't just hammer out a quick email and press send. Craft it so the firm you contact perceives you as a serious candidate. Say something like this:

"Hello, my name is [*insert name*]. I am a student in [*insert CFP® certification program*]. I am seeking a paid internship for the summer. I have been researching firms in the area, and based on [*insert items of interest*], your business stood out to me. Here are some things I think I could do to help add value to your team during a possible internship with your firm:

- Work with website platform WordPress and a web designer to update your website

- Help strategize and deploy digital marketing/social media marketing strategies

- Research and evaluate software vendors under consideration

- Produce meeting prep materials and assist in post client meeting implementation of recommendations

- Be available for all-around support for Associate Planner and Lead Planners, for any admin/ops, client service task they may need

- Review and rework, if necessary, all written marketing materials

- Input data into financial planning software

- Greet clients and make them comfortable when they come in for in-person meetings

- *[insert any other areas you feel strongly about but be cautious not to put something down if you can't deliver on]*

I have some additional thoughts on adding value that I would like to discuss with you. I have attached my resume, an article I wrote about the profession's future, and a project I completed in one of my classes so you can get a sense of my work product.

I will call you at [insert time] next week to follow up and discuss this further. Thank you for your time and consideration.

If you have any questions or want to chat before then, I can be reached at email@youremailaddress.com and cell at XXX-XXX-XXXX.

Sincerely,

[insert name]

Now you have given a reason and a heads up for calling the firm, so it would be a warm call and not a cold call out of the blue, which is not as effective.

Here's some inside information about email communication: *avoid vanity email addresses.* Emails like nolegirl@gmail.com or pgatourpro@gmail.com are a turnoff. Keep it simple and professional, like FirstLastname@whateverdomain.com; if you are worried about privacy, use it only for job-seeking purposes.

Then put a reminder in your calendar to follow up with them via phone five to seven days later and say something like this:

Hello, *[appropriate salutation and last name]*. My name is *[insert name]*, and I am a student in *[insert CFP® certification program]*. I am seeking a paid internship for the summer.

I sent you an email last *[insert exact day and time]*. Did you receive it? I have been following your firm for some time now and would love to learn from you while adding value to your organization. Do you have any projects for which no one seems to have time?

You will probably end up leaving a voicemail. Your voicemail script can be similar to the above. Make sure you write it out and practice it a few times so you don't start with "uh" and "um." If they answer, you need to deliver a concise and compelling first few sentences so they can hear the passion and conviction in your voice about why this is the profession for you and how you want to help people and assist their firm.

Remember, decision-makers are inundated with people contacting them for the same opportunity you seek. What will set you apart from the rest? Being a person who demonstrates effort, takes the initiative, shows some grit, and displays the courage to put themselves out there. Firm owners have difficulty saying "No" to people with these qualities. Make it easy for them to say "Yes" and hard for them to say "No."

If you must leave a voicemail, wait for another three to five days, then call again. If you don't hear anything back, take that as a sign they do not want to proceed and note their nonresponse on your tracking sheet. What's a tracking sheet? Good question. It's a sheet or journal you should create to keep track of your outreach efforts. I have included a sample in Chapter 4 materials.

Once you note their name, firm, and nonresponse, add them to an email drip campaign list that you will use later and move on to the next firm. Not getting a response is unprofessional, but don't take it personally. One of the most valuable traits you need to develop as an aspiring financial planner and human living on this earth is to bounce back after rejection.

Now, if you do enough outreach and work the avenues we have discussed to their fullest extent, you could end up with a few firms interested in you. Congratulations! This puts you in an ideal situation to pick the best one. Here are some questions to help you better understand the opportunity to evaluate which is right for you:

Have you had an internship previously?

You are trying to understand whether they have a formal recurring internship, if this is the first time, or somewhere in between. Firms that have hosted interns previously are more likely to have the systems and procedures in place for you to have a good experience.

On the other hand, plenty of firms have never had an intern but would still provide a great opportunity. If you are the first intern, do everything you can to ensure they have a good experience so they will hire you for a full-time permanent position. If they consider your internship successful and helpful to their firm, they will hire interns in the following years. One of your projects could be to document your work/projects and create a mini curriculum that can be used regularly each year. I know it might be extra work, but go ahead and suggest it and knock your boss's socks off!

Who will be my supervisor?

You need to know to whom you go with questions. It may not be the person that hired you. When I was an intern, the person who hired me failed to communicate with their team that I was at their disposal. I found out later they were all hesitant to assign me to work because they didn't know they had that authority.

Will I have the opportunity to listen in on client meetings?

If you want to be a client-facing financial planner, I encourage you to strive for this. Some firms may not go for it, so you need to be sensitive. However, many firms will let you observe in a client meeting.

Some firms will say their clients aren't comfortable with an intern listening in on sensitive discussions around their finances. But I've found the opposite, as people generally like having a larger audience when talking about themselves. Plus, they usually want newer and/or younger people to succeed, whether they know you or not.

What projects would you like for me to work on?

Organizations have a backlog of projects they're too busy to get to. They should have these listed and available. Assuming the projects are things an intern can do, working on them allows you to add value to a firm while learning the business.

If you have had any business management or practice management courses in your CFP® program, you should already know what potential bottlenecks and pain points firms face. So, leverage this knowledge when discussing your project list. It may be moving data between software programs or a new custodian or broker-dealer.

All of it is important work. But everyone else is too busy for it. You can wow a firm if you can identify challenges, develop a solution to remedy the challenge, and then execute the strategy. You might consider this a high standard for which to strive but realize that is what you will be asked to do in your role as an Associate Financial Planner for the firm.

What is the pay range for this internship?

You should be targeting paid internships. The pay we see, depending on geographical area, ranges anywhere from $10–$30 per hour. You will be in good shape if you find something in that area. Researching the cost of living in certain areas using a site like Sperling's Best Places https://www.bestplaces.net/docs/datasource.aspx to help determine what you need to ask for in compensation and to have data to justify your request.

You may not get everything you want depending on the job market. You need to go into this like anything else and list all your "Must haves" and "Nice to haves."

You can stick to your guns, but realistically, you should take it if you can find someone who will offer a solid opportunity. At this point in your career, it is all about getting started, even if you aren't granted every wish on your internship list.

The Story of My Internship

Here is how I secured my internship when I broke into the financial planning profession.

As a student in the Texas Tech University Financial Planning program, I was required to intern at a financial planning firm to graduate. The internship course at that time was only offered once per year, so if I did not secure a paid internship for course credit, I would have to wait an entire year before I could retake the class and then graduate.

The timing was unfortunate because it was about eight months after the terrorist attacks of September 11, 2001. The Dow Jones industrial average was at ~9,500, down from 11,000 before 9/11. It was a perfect storm of the tech bubble and a terrorist attack that disrupted our economy and the stock market. I was a 21-year-old college student that had little to offer. I had no existing book of business, couldn't generate revenue by bringing in new clients, and did not possess the technical knowledge of certain planning areas to work with clients right off the bat unsupervised.

Firm revenues were down, people were panicking, and financial planning firms were laying off people. It wasn't the best time to convince someone to take on the cost of paying me and training me for three months. I needed an action plan.

Setting the Action Plan

I knew enough to know that I did not have the best GPA, wasn't the most polished communicator, nor the most analytical. So I had to get creative. Here is what I did.

I knew most of my peers were returning to their Texas hometowns: Dallas/Ft Worth, Houston, Austin, and San Antonio. I did not target these areas because I knew the competition would be fierce. Plus, I wanted to get out of my comfort zone and explore different areas of the country too.

I have always tried to approach things in my life and career by putting myself in as many win-win situations as possible. My thought was to find a fun and exciting area of the country to spend a summer in case my internship turned out to be a bust.

I listed all the places that met these criteria: San Francisco, Chicago, Seattle, and New York. I had New Zealand on the list too. It ended up not working out. But I challenge you to shoot for the stars.

I ended up targeting the San Francisco Bay Area because I had never been there and had heard from a family member who lived there that it doesn't get hot during the summer—every Texan's dream!

Now that I had the area I wanted to target, I had to find firms to contact. I did some digging on the internet and found links to two magazines after I typed "Best financial planners in San Francisco." The magazines were *Medical Economics* and *Worth's Top Advisors of the Year*.

I purchased hard copies of these magazines since I was not a subscriber. Then, I input all the San Francisco Bay Area financial planners on those two lists into a spreadsheet. There were about thirty-five firms on both of those lists that met my geographical requirement, so I started doing my research on each firm.

I went to their websites, read their newsletters, and pulled their form ADV from the SEC website (https://adviserinfo.sec.gov/) to try and learn as much as possible about them. This research helped me determine if they fit my skill set well. I wasn't interested in the size of the firm. I wanted to know if they focused on financial planning and whether the planners held the CFP® certification. Through my research, I narrowed it down to about thirty firms.

You can find lists of financial planners in financial publications such as Barron's, Forbes, and Investment News, among others. But be aware just because someone is on that list doesn't necessarily mean they are a great financial planner. Many lists allow self-nominations and tend to highlight the largest and fastest-growing firms.

You can also connect with me to find employers. Once you connect with me, this will give you access to my network with thousands of connections and potential employers and mentors. *Note:* Find me on LinkedIn at https://www.linkedin.com/in/calebbrowncfp/. Scan here to make my network your network.

What Was I Going to Offer?

I had to think long and hard about what I would say to these firms since the economy had tanked, and I brought little to the table. I knew my peers and competitors would send the standard materials to prospective firms: resume and cover letter. I considered differentiating myself so employers would remember me even if my credentials were not as good as my peers.

I decided to print hard copies of my resume, mission, and values statement, an article that someone had written highlighting my financial planning program, and an assignment I had completed for my retirement planning course. I packaged this information into individual legal pad-sized mailers and mailed them to all the California firms on my list. Here is a sample checklist I used:

Organization	ABC Financial	
Contact - Name	Mary Smith	
Contact - Phone	888-888-8888	
Contact - Email	mary@abcfinancial.com	
Target clientele	Pre-retirees	
# of team members	8	
# of CFP®s	4	
# of clients	300	
Assets Under Mgmt	250MM	
Date Package Sent	01/01/XX	
Follow up Call Held	01/08/XX	
Status	Interested	
Next Step	Video Call	

I then called each firm precisely one week after sending out the mailing. I hoped the firms would receive and review my package before I called them. You can pay a little extra for tracking when you ship them, so you have the exact date and time the package was delivered. This helped me a few times when some firms said they had not received my package. They didn't end up hiring me but did compliment me on my organization and attention to detail.

Next, I had to pick up the phone and make a warm call to these busy professionals. Targeting a time of day when folks are in the office, not at lunch, is a good idea. So, I targeted early afternoon, just after lunchtime, when I thought most planners would be back in their offices and available.

Making the call was a nerve-wracking experience. Butterflies galore. But I kept to the script I shared earlier in the chapter and was able to stumble through the first few calls. Then, after a few calls, things started to flow more naturally. One-third of the firms I called did not return my call, even after I had called twice and followed up via email.

You will get rejected like this. Be prepared for it, and don't take it personally.

What I came to realize many years later was that if the firm was not open to speaking with me for a few minutes about their business and a profession they loved, the internship wouldn't have been a fit for me either.

Another third said they'd received my mailer but hadn't had time to review it. I put this group on a "follow-up" list with the plan to reach out to them the following week. Are you seeing a pattern here with how often I used and continue to use lists? Lists empower you to be a person who takes the initiative, follows up, and remembers important events. That's impressive to hiring firms, and they will remember.

The remaining ten firms had reviewed the material and took my phone call, but most said they were not hiring. A few even said they were closing up shop and retiring due to the drop in revenue they had experienced from the stock market decline. Experiencing these calls and subsequent rejections early on in my career gave me a much-needed dose of humility. Calls like that are hard, but they shaped my character and gave me a little extra grit and some thicker skin I needed to develop.

Persistence Pays Off

I finally got someone on the phone who would listen to me. But they couldn't move forward due to financial reasons. My list was shrinking. I was feeling depressed and feared that I'd failed.

But I kept following my process. I remained positive. I contacted a few more firms. But nothing.

Then, finally, I had a breakthrough.

One of the firms responded to a follow-up email I sent a few days earlier.

"We like the information you put together for us. No one has ever done that, but we have already committed to an intern for the summer. However, I would like to have a short phone call with you to learn a little more about what you are looking for to see if we can point you in the right direction."

There was light at the end of the tunnel! I scheduled a call with this firm owner, Norman (Norm) Boone, and was super excited I had someone to talk to. One important note to remember when scheduling with firm owners is to schedule around them—take whatever times they give you and make them work. Avoid saying something like, 'Oh, I can't do that time...' or 'That doesn't work for me...' or 'I've got another meeting then, can you do this time?' You ask busy firm owners for their valuable time, so make it easy for them!

I emphasized my passion for the profession and commitment to the career on the call. My zeal paid off. After that conversation, the firm owner sent me five names of fellow planners in his study group and told me to reach out to each of them and use his name as a reference.

After emailing the first two names on the list, I had two interviews scheduled and two solid opportunities. I had one phone interview with each, discussing the position's responsibilities, logistics, and compensation. (FYI, an additional compensation note—I was paid $15/hr. To intern for the firm in California.) After that, I narrowed my list down to my top firm run by Larry Ginsburg.

The direct referral changed the game for me immediately. The owners on the list given to me knew if their colleague vouched for me, then I was worth talking to. I did not fully understand the gravity of this until much later in my career. Somehow, I convinced Norm to have confidence in me and trust that I would not make him look bad for recommending me. The entire financial planning career is built upon this, getting clients to trust you even when they have not known you for very long. If you can get people to trust you, you will be successful.

One of the goals I had for my internship was to observe a client meeting. I remember feeling nervous about asking Larry about it. I was scared he'd deny my request, and I would have to start the entire process over. But he welcomed the idea and even mentioned wanting me to be exposed to all areas of the firm during my tenure.

I loaded up my car and headed to California, not knowing what to expect. Stay tuned for more about what you can expect in an internship and my experience.

Tips for Acing Your First Day as An Intern

We know that starting a new position can be one of the most exciting times in your life and one of the most anxious. See the tips below for preparing for your first day on the job so you don't stress and can enjoy this great moment and be prepared to knock it out of the park!

Tip #1 — Show up early

If you are commuting, check Waze or your app of choice the night before your first day. Enter the time you aim to arrive so it will factor in peak traffic times. Add at least 30 minutes to the time it states. Realize you will have plenty to do if you arrive early.

And how cool would it be if you arrived first and had to wait on someone to open the door? Remember, if you are a few minutes early, no one remembers. They only remember if you are late or very early! If you are working virtually, get to your desk early and send everyone a

"*Good morning, team—I'm so glad to be here! I can't wait to get started*"
message.

Tip #2 — Dress above expectations

Always go for a professional business look. Keep in mind you can always remove jackets, ties, etc. Also, don't eat breakfast and brush your teeth with work clothes. People remember those pesky stains that you may have missed. You don't want to look disheveled. If you bring an extra blouse, shirt, etc., you won't have to worry about this derailing a perfect day.

Tip #3 — Pack lunch

Most firms will take you out for your first day or two but don't expect it. Maybe they have plans to take you somewhere. Perhaps everyone goes out. But you don't want to be stuck without lunch. If the firm does not take you out, or no one invites you out (probably not a good sign, frankly), reach out to a co-worker and invite them to eat with you.

Tip #4 — Bring your tools for success

Plan to show up with your financial calculator, a few pens, and a paper notebook for notes. You must write down everything anyone says because they expect you to remember. They may not have the processes and procedures in place for your reference. Your notes could become the new processes and procedures manual and CRM workflows.

Don't plan to decorate your office on day one. Do that later on your own time. If you own a tablet or laptop, consider bringing that in your bag in case something happens with the procurement and setup of your workstation.

Tip #5 — Bring a voided check

Depending on the firm's size, you could spend most of your first day with the HR/Benefits team setting up your payroll, direct deposit, and benefits. Show them you can anticipate and are always thinking ahead of the process. You will be their new best friend if you have all your documentation.

Furthermore, know your tax situation and complete your form beforehand at https://www.irs.gov/pub/irs-pdf/fw4.pdf. Nothing looks worse than a financial planner in training who doesn't know their way around basic tax documents.

Tip #6 — Wash and clean your vehicle

Whether you like it or not, you are representing the firm. You never know who you will see or when the boss or client might need a ride.

***

Hopefully, these tips will prove helpful to you and reduce some of the first-day jitters. Remember, it's okay to have some nervousness because you want to put your best foot forward. Everyone experiences this—it's natural. If that doesn't help, realize that this firm saw something in you and wants to put your valuable skills to use in their organization.

Key Takeaways

- Speak up for what you want. Don't waste time trying to guess how people are going to react.

- Think outside the box when trying to differentiate yourself.

- Expand your horizons and push yourself out of your comfort zone.

- Develop a process and stay organized.

- Keep your head down and stay persistent and positive when facing setbacks.

Action Items

- Review Chapter 4 Materials using this QR Code.

- Create and/or update your resume.

- Develop a cover letter or summary statement.

- Establish and/or update your LinkedIn profile. Connect with me on LinkedIn.

- Write down four things you would like to do in your internship.

- Use the script I provided or create your own. Practice it at least twice aloud, then record it on your smartphone. Play it back for yourself and listen for areas that need to be improved. If you are like me, you probably dread listening to your voice, so this might be challenging. You can do it, though!

CHAPTER 5

— · —

WHAT TO EXPECT FROM YOUR INTERNSHIP

"Education is what remains after one has forgotten what one has learned in school."
—Albert Einstein

By this point, you should be well on your way to obtaining your degree. I don't mean to diminish your schooling; it is very important. But book knowledge means nothing unless it is applied. The knowledge you receive from a good internship experience is invaluable when starting as a financial planner. In this chapter, I will sketch out what you can expect from your internship. Remember, you aren't going to know everything, and that is okay! Capitalize on the resourcefulness you have learned through your educational career. During your sophomore or junior year, start a document that is easily accessible so you can begin to build out a list of planning resources (see the resources section for Chapter 5 for a list to get you started), such as irs.gov, ERISA limits for the year, other helpful articles and calculators, insurance premium estimators, etc. These resources will make you shine during your internship and add more value when solving client problems and answering questions, and there is a chance the firm you work for may not have it.

You want to do everything possible to ensure a valuable internship experience. Your firm should have some pre-planned projects for you to work on so you can add value and learn multiple aspects of the business.

If your host firm does not have a clear list of projects for you or you run out of things to work on, consider taking these ideas to your supervisors.

Document processes, sequences, and procedures

This is a no-brainer if you are new and talking to everyone, trying to figure out what everyone does. Remember my previous note about writing lists and keeping track of things? That applies here, too. Write it all down, and/or record it via audio, for future interns and other employees' job descriptions. This is the first step in transforming a practice into a business.

Compare various software packages

Depending on how far you are through your coursework, you might have had prior exposure to financial planning software packages. Show them what you know, especially if the firm is considering adding financial planning software or is looking to make a change. Provide input on software decisions by writing up a recommendation on which program you would choose for the firm based on what you know about them.

Develop newsletter and/or add to existing content

For firms that don't subscribe to pre-packaged newsletter content services, this can be a good way for you to add value since searching for content is rarely a good use of a senior planner's time. Review past newsletters to see the content, style, and flow, then go and find relevant content. This is a great chance to use your knowledge and experience with AI tools like ChatGPT.

Participate in client meetings

It is much easier for senior advisors to run a client meeting and focus on the client when they don't have to worry about taking notes. Sit in on client meetings with your senior advisor. Yes, both new and existing clients.

Many firms provide this opportunity to their interns because it will help solidify your choice of and passion for financial planning and your intern sponsor's confidence in you. Understand that you will mostly be in an observer and note-taker role. Ask to update the meeting process flow chart if current materials are outdated and need a refresher.

Help with quarterly reporting

Sending out quarterly reports is a time-intensive process. There are many tools now that automate most of this function. But, if firms are not utilizing those tools, having an extra pair of hands can be helpful here.

Help your firm print, staple, and mail the reports. This isn't the most glamorous work, but it's important to many firms' operations, so don't think you are above it.

What everyone else does not want to do

Interns should be exposed to all aspects of the firm. That means the good, the bad, and the ugly. You must understand that client meetings are not the only function of an advisory firm. It's important for firms to keep a running list of tasks that no one wants to do. The right intern will attack that list with great enthusiasm.

"Our internship program is very competitive. We typically hire 3-4 per year and it is immensely valuable to our firm to have the extra help, but we also use it as an extended job interview too for those we want to bring onto the team permanently."

—Shannon T., RIA firm owner in the Midwest

A Day in The Life of an Intern

Most internships are structured like a typical eight-to-five Monday through Friday job, especially during the summer. However, since these positions tend to be shorter temporary types, they are more project-based.

Also, there will be daily work activities such as helping the planning staff complete pre and post-client meetings to do's, performing investment research, ordering supplies, updating client relationship management (CRM) software, inputting data into financial planning software, observing client meetings and phone calls with senior planners, managing social media accounts, updating the firm website, scanning documents, and contacting clients for updated information.

Here are a few examples of how your day as an intern could be structured.

Example 1

8:00 a.m.—Attend All Team Weekly Planning Meetings

9:30–11:00—Post new article to the website, update social media content, send Smiths an article about upcoming Greece vacation

11:30–12:30 p.m.—Lunch with Associate Planner

1–3:00—Scan and file new client information

3–3:30—Listen in on conference call with the Johnsons

4–6:00 p.m.—Review client account beneficiary designations for any omissions or errors

Example 2

10:00–11:30—Flex time between departments

12:00 p.m.—Prepare new paperwork for custodian change over

2–3:00—Review Google Analytics with Operations manager

3:30–5:30 p.m.—Research Socially Responsible Exchange Traded Funds for Associate Planner for Peterson account

Example 3

8:30–11:00 a.m.—Software conversion and manual data scrub project

11:30–12:00 p.m.—Lunch

12:30–2:30—Reorganizing A–D client file structure

3–4:30 p.m.—Set up Facebook Ads for new marketing campaign

Example 4

8:30–10:00 a.m.—Observe Plan Presentation Meeting with the Wilsons

10:30–11:00—Debrief with Senior Planner on Wilson meeting

11–12:00 p.m.—Lunch with Operations Manager

12:30–1:30—Help Associate Planner Prepare agenda and reports for Dickson Meeting

2–4:00—Observe and take notes in the Dickson meeting

4:30–5:30—Debrief with Associate Planner on Dickson meeting

5:30–6:00 p.m.—Document Dickson meeting notes into CRM

What to Do If Your Internship Isn't Going as Planned

I had driven 1,500 miles for my internship, so I had high expectations and wanted the best experience possible. It started slowly, primarily due to the team needing to prepare for my arrival. I knew the firm had an intern previously, but there was a lot of scrambling going on when I first arrived. I had to wait several days for my computer, email, office access, etc., to be set up. Ideally, all that would have been done before my arrival, but I understood everyone was busy, and setting up for me would be pulling them away from their daily work. I worked mainly with the Associate Financial Planner, Senior Financial Planner, and the administrative team members to learn various aspects of the business. They spent time showing me how the firm operated; however, after a few weeks, I was getting a bit frustrated and disappointed that I could not work on anything to help them, and I knew I was creating extra work for them. I also spent very little time with Larry, who hired me.

So after a month of this, I approached Larry and said I wanted to be more involved in helping the team and spend more time with him directly so he could mentor me. Very professionally and firmly, he reminded me that he had a business to run and was busy during the 8–5 workday period he was paying me for. I got it and understood where he was coming from, so I suggested that I clock out as usual at 5 pm and offered to stay around the office for a few hours when his day ended at 6:30–7 pm if he would spend a few minutes with me debriefing on the day. I don't think he expected me to follow through with it because he agreed, so we did this for a few weeks, and it was the turning point I sought.

After a few weeks of this, he invited me to grab a bite to eat with him before he headed home. We shared several meals over the coming weeks. Then one evening, he asked if I would like to go to COSTCO with him so he could pick up some office supplies. I went with him, and we walked around the store talking about all sorts of stuff, from business to personal life. It was great! He would share his challenges and what he was working on and coach me on effectively dealing with people to help me get the desired outcomes. We did this several times, and I looked forward to these outings.

One Saturday, he asked me to come to his golf club and play golf with him. We had a great time golfing, but he also introduced me to his fellow members, and we chatted about someone he was targeting to become a client. This person had recently sold a business and had a financial planner but would have made a good client for Larry's firm, so we discussed how to approach the situation.

Things were turning around; I couldn't believe all the time he was spending with me and the valuable mentoring I was receiving. I only had a few weeks left in my internship, and he invited me to his home to have dinner with his family. This was another great experience because I could observe how he interacted with his family, and it meant a lot to me that he would bring me into his personal life when he didn't have to.

At the end of my internship, I was exposed to all the main areas of a firm, including operations, investments, financial planning, and client service. I learned the most from spending time with my boss at dinner, trips to COSTCO, the golf course, and all our other time outside the office. It was also a bonus that he took me to a study group meeting where he and about a dozen other planners discussed ways to improve their business for an entire day. He also paid for me to go to a Naviplan software training with the rest of his team.

Many other financial planners want to provide an opportunity like this for you, but it will probably not fall into your lap. With careful planning and hustle, you can also have a once-in-a-lifetime internship experience.

I Cannot Find an Internship; Now What?

Finding an internship can be difficult because many financial planning firms, especially smaller companies, sometimes need help to see the value in an intern. You need to know that some firm owners see interns as a headache, hassle, and waste of time. So, it would help if you went above and beyond to convey your value to them. And then you need to deliver on the value you promised when you arrive at their firm.

Please keep in mind firm owners typically see the larger revenue-producing items such as bringing in clients, leading and managing relationships, and giving advice as the most valuable areas in which to invest their time and resources. Most interns can't do these things yet.

But you will get there!

Don't let this discourage you.

But you need to be aware of how many firms view interns. You might even encounter a firm telling you to get an internship elsewhere and then come back to them once you have experience. How frustrating, right? But don't let it deter you from pursuing your dream career.

Here are more ideas to try if you are struggling to find an internship:

Expand your search radius

The major metropolitan areas contain the most firms. So focus on those areas first. If you aren't interested in places like San Francisco, New York, or Chicago, you might also consider looking for virtual internship opportunities. I targeted San Francisco for my internship and, at that time, there were lots of firms for me to reach out to. If you are trying to go back close to your home in Small Town, USA there might not be as many firms to choose from.

I also encourage you to get out of your comfort zone. If you can swing it financially, go somewhere different and strive for a rich experience outside of work as well. Try to experience as many different cultures, varying paces of life, and geographical regions as possible. This will make you a better planner and a more well-rounded person.

Consider other channels

If you have your heart set on an internship with a wirehouse and are striking out, look at the other channels, such as RIAs and insurance companies.

Consider unpaid opportunities

You should always get paid for your time and labor. If you can receive course credit, taking an unpaid opportunity is more palpable, but still not ideal.

Look at part-time positions

A full-time, three-month internship would be 500 hours of work time. Firms may not want to commit to that much time or only have room in the budget for a part-time worker who isn't generating revenue.

Secure an externship

An externship is similar to an internship but shorter. Due to their abbreviated length, this might work better for your schedule and your host firms. It also lessens their commitment because some firms might have fears of having an intern and keeping them busy for three months versus a couple of weeks. Financial planner Hannah Moore, has created a virtual externship that is reasonably priced at $299. You can find more information here: https://amplifiedplanning.com/externship/

Seek mentors

You always want to be forthright with your intentions. Still, if you are having difficulty convincing someone to hire you as an intern, you might try to reposition the conversation as you are seeking a mentor. Busy firm owners are more likely to commit to this since their time and financial outlay wouldn't be as stressed. Then you would need to work on wowing your mentor, and who knows, it could turn into an internship or apprenticeship situation.

Get aggressive

Make sure your LinkedIn profile always states your intentions, "New financial planning graduate actively seeking an internship."

Leverage social media

Send out a message on your social platforms—"Financial Planning student in need of an internship."

Utilize print media

Some of you may be saying what is that? But it does still exist. Write an article about the difficulties of getting hired as an intern and send it to industry publications such as Barrons, Investment News, Financial Planning, Journal of Financial Planning, etc.

You also can consider programs such as the BLX Internship, Planning Zoo, and Amplified Planning. The BLX internship program was designed to help people who identify as Black and Latinx get their foot in the door to the financial planning profession. You can find out more and apply at https://blxinternship.org/.

Planning Zoo was created to provide more opportunities for aspiring financial planners to learn how to do financial planning in a part-time, virtual, flexible, and paid environment. This program is specially designed for students and recent graduates of CFP® certification programs that are focused on learning the craft of financial planning from the technical and software perspective. Ideal candidates are new planners pursuing CFP® certification, looking to gain qualifying experience hours while working with real-life cases and learning current financial planning software. You can learn more at https://planningzoo.com/.

Amplified Planning was designed to give new and experienced planners alike a way to see behind the curtain on what goes on in client meetings. This is another training resource developed by Hannah Moore, CFP® who records her client meetings and makes the videos available to watch, learn, and practice various exercises and quizzes to help in the advice delivery functions of the financial planner's job. You can learn more here: https://amplifiedplanning.com/

Securing Great Mentors

Ideally, you will have a phenomenal internship experience and gain multiple ongoing mentors. You have a better chance of getting to where you want to go professionally if you have several mentors who will help guide you along the way. I can't stress the importance of mentors enough. Mentors will give you insight into the profession as no book or tutorial can. Make it your priority to come under the tutelage of a great mentor.

Some mentor connection places like FPA Nexgen, NAPFA Genesis Groups, and the CFP Board already exist, so start there. But don't be shy about reaching out to well-known planners in your area or ones you see in industry publications. Call them directly, tell them your story, and ask if they would be open to mentoring you.

Talking about mentors reminds me of another great thing about financial planning. Many successful financial planners are available to spend time helping new planners even if they can't hire them for an intern or Associate Planner position. Here's the important thing about setting up a mentoring relationship. It would help if you took the initiative to lay out how you see the mentorship going.

Where many new planners fall short is they get a very busy firm owner to mentor them and then don't take any action, hoping that the busy firm owner will do all the work. Don't make this mistake! If you aren't sure what a good mentorship relationship looks like, check out *The Heart of Mentoring* By David Stoddard.

Here are some things a good mentor will do for you.

Provide Inspiration and Constructive Coaching

A good mentor will be open to you so you know what their career path looked like, their mistakes, and how difficult it was to get to where they are today. You get a good framework for how to or not to model your career and a greater understanding of how their career looks currently. One mentor I had who was very direct, took a tough love approach and had lots of constructive criticisms; saw me do a mock presentation and told me I was terrific and should leverage my speaking skills. I couldn't believe it as I was beginning to think everything I did was wrong.

Take a Genuine Interest in Your Career and Life

They should ask you from time to time about something non-work related that is important to you. Initially, they might try something as simple as approaching you and asking how you're doing. Like all good relationships, it goes both ways. As you learn from them, they should also be getting to know what is important to you. Another mentor would listen to my phone calls and coach me. They also helped me respond to emails clients would send, improving my communication skills substantially.

Listen to You As They Listen to Their Clients

Most planners do a wonderful job listening to and managing their clients. Your mentor should take this same approach with you. Look for them to make you comfortable to share your ideas openly. This is a crucial component of a successful long-term relationship. They should strive to create an environment where groupthink doesn't rule, and all ideas are encouraged and considered equally.

Invest the time

How fast you progress up the career ladder depends a lot on you, but it also depends a lot on the people surrounding you. If they prioritize spending time with you, you will recognize the investment they are making and want to stay working with them for the long term. Furthermore, word spreads quickly in our tight-knit profession about firms that mentor their employees excellently.

Here is a sample script for approaching a potential mentor:

Hello [Title. Last Name],

It was great to meet you at [insert conference/event] [or I saw you present or in _____ magazine and learned a lot from you]. I admire your dedication to your clients and the success you have achieved in your career.

I am an early career planner. I am seeking experienced successful planners in our great profession to help me navigate my career. I would love to be able to call and/or email you from time to time to ask for your advice. Are you open to it if I check in with you periodically? If not, do you know someone else who could take a few minutes with me every quarter?

Thank you so much for considering my request. I appreciate your time and contributions to our profession. Please let me know if you have any questions or if there is anything I can do for you.

Sincerely, [Your Full Name]

Key Takeaways

- Your internship doesn't have to be with the perfect firm; instead, start building your career's bedrock sooner rather than later.

- Focus on how you will add value to your internship hosting firm.

- You may have to drive more of the internship experience than anticipated if the firm is unprepared.

- The right mentor(s) will get you to where you want to go much faster than solely on your own.

- Try to complete as many internships as you can before graduation.

Action Items

- Review Chapter 5 Materials using this QR Code.

- Read David Stoddard's *The Heart of Mentoring: Ten Proven Principles for Developing People to Their Fullest Potential.*

- Reach out to at least two firms you might want to intern with; if they don't take you as an intern, ask them to be your mentor.

- Write down at least three things you would like from a mentor.

CHAPTER 6

— · —

SECURING FULL-TIME EMPLOYMENT AS A FINANCIAL PLANNER

"Your talent determines what you can do. Your motivation determines how much you are willing to do. Your attitude determines how well you do it."

—Lou Holtz

So, how do you leap from an intern to a full-time financial planner? Well, it begins with a plan. Benjamin Franklin said, *"By failing to prepare, you are preparing to fail."* Don't approach your career as a financial planner with nonchalance. Planning requires intentionality and a good bit of forethought, and resiliency. You've got to put in the work now to secure success in the future.

Let's look at how to develop a solid game plan as you consider transitioning into your full-time financial planner career.

Finding a Firm to Start Your Career

After I completed my internship, I returned to school for one last semester before I graduated. It was a hectic time because I had to secure a part-time job, take two of the hardest classes in the financial planning major, and begin trying to find a full-time permanent job after graduation, only a few months away. I could already feel the walls caving in as I drove my car back from California after a successful internship experience.

While going to school full-time, here is how I secured part-time employment in the profession during my last semester. I did a simple internet search for financial planners near me and had about twenty firms to consider. Since I was short on time and faced a serious case of FOMO due to everyone else already having something lined up after graduation, I took the same packet I had put together and mailed it to secure my internship and drove to each organization's office. Yes! Twenty different offices. I knew leaving it with someone at the front desk wasn't the best option, so I always asked if the firm owner was available. I was only able to speak to two firm owners out of the twenty firms, and they weren't hiring.

About two weeks went by, and I was certainly feeling the pressure now, total déjà vu, and then I got a call from one of the companies I had visited and dropped off my materials. They were looking for someone to work for a few hours each week with the firm founder on how they could begin offering more financial planning to their legacy insurance clientele. I had no idea what I was getting into but was desperate, so I accepted the position. The offer was $12/hr. plus 10% of commissions I generated or helped generate. Not long after I started, though, the founder had a major health issue, and I did not get to work with him much. I was fully expecting to be laid off, but I went ahead and developed a proposal of how I could still add value to the other insurance agents in the firm. The firm that I went to work for was an insurance agency focused on selling life insurance and annuity products to retirees.

I was shocked when they mentioned they would keep me around, and I worked there for about nine months until I graduated. I did everything from making copies, cleaning files, performing analyses, meeting with clients in the office, sorting out client insurance policy issues, contacting various insurance company call centers, visiting clients at their homes, and helping the founder's son brainstorm ideas to generate more revenue. They even gave me my own office, which worked out great when I started studying for the CFP® exam! I could close the door and focus. I was in my early twenties, and everyone I worked with was in their sixties or older. Here are a few things I learned from my time there:

1. You can learn a lot from experienced professionals from their stories about their successes and failures.

2. If you listen, genuinely care, and act in a kind and professional manner, you will gain respect no matter how much more experience they have.

3. Insights on how to get people to take action when they do not necessarily want to.

4. It was my first time in an office environment, which helped me tremendously when transitioning to an RIA after taking the CFP® exam.

In developing a plan for your career, one of the chief characteristics you want to strive for is clarity. All great plans, whether career plans or plans in battle, require clarity of mind and action. Below I've sketched out fifteen elements to consider as you begin your career as a financial planner. Some will be weightier than others. But all are important components of searching for the perfect firm for you as you embark on your career journey.

These elements will help you ask the right questions, clearly defining what you want and should expect. Consider this list as a guiding rubric you can reference while searching for a firm. This set of elements will keep you from saying yes to a potentially bad situation and help you remember what will be expected of you.

Element #1 — Develop a Plan

Starting your career in financial planning can be overwhelming. Similar to what you did for your internship, before you start searching for a position, establish a list of your non-negotiables and negotiable things when reviewing a particular career opportunity. It's easier to get into the right fit if you have taken the time to think through extensively what you're seeking before you dive in headfirst.

Element #2 — Goals

All great plans begin with a set of goals. They drive the plan. In the same way, we map out a financial plan for our clients; you'll need to identify your personal career goals before developing a plan to achieve them. Consider some basic questions, such as these, to help clarify your goals.

Why did you choose this profession?

Do you want to become a lead planner?

Do you want to do sales or business development?

Do you see yourself managing a team in the future?

How do you want to interact with clients?

Do you see yourself becoming a partner in a firm?

With financial planning as your career, the possibilities are endless. But endless possibilities can also breed confusion. Take the time, get specific with your goals, and write them down! Psychologists have proven that you are much more likely to achieve your goals if you simply write them down. Aspiring financial planners are most successful when they develop clarity around future goals and expectations in writing. Ultimately, you have to be the one to set your own goals, and it can be challenging because you don't want to put them too low and give yourself a false sense of accomplishment or set them too high and give yourself a false sense of failure.

Here are some sample goals to help get your thought process started:

Short-term goals — 0–1 year

- Secure full-time paid position with fee-based RIA

- Pass Securities Industry Essentials (SIE) exam

- Pass Series 7 exam

- Pass Series 65 exam

- Learn all clients that I am backup point of contact for

- Complete 12 financial plans in firm's financial planning software

- Sit in at least 30 client meetings

- Bring one client to the firm

Mid-range goals — 1–3 years

- Pass CFP® certification exam

- Secure promotion to Associate Financial Planner

- Serve as Lead Planner for A and AA clients

- Take lead and run Discovery (data gathering) meetings

- Present on at least 2 agenda items in Plan Presentation meetings

- Visit Alma Mater and speak to students about the profession and my role

- Earn at least $75,000 per year

<u>Long-term goals</u> — 3+ years
- Enroll in Masters of Financial Planning program

- Secure promotion to Lead Planner position

- Bring in at least 1 client per month

- Supervise interns and new Associate program

- Develop expertise in charitable giving

- Become an equity owner

To help further, ask yourself this question if you feel you are getting stuck: "What must happen for me to look back on my first few years and say the journey thus far has been successful?"

Element #3 — Firm

The firm you join will have a lasting impact on your planning knowledge, philosophies, and career satisfaction. Finding the right firm is important, and much goes into discovering it. But don't let that overwhelm you. The perfect firm for you may not exist right now. So don't stress if you can't seem to find it.

Think about the size of the firm you want to join. Large and small firms vary drastically. As firms get larger, there is increased training and structure but less flexibility and potential to impact change. Smaller firms tend to provide exposure a lot quicker. If you are considering relocation, consider if you would prefer a large firm where you can meet other people or if you can build a social network outside of the office.

Element #4 — Location

Speaking of relocation, what are your thoughts on where you want to be? Or does it even matter since there are virtual positions available as well? Location is important. The locations you target will have a substantial impact on the number and quality of opportunities available. Areas with which you are familiar and have familial ties are the safer options and less risky for a firm owner to hire you into.

But you should also consider expanding your horizons. Take a shot at something new. But understand that with less familiarity you have in an area, the greater the risk assumed by the firm owner. If you live on the east coast and have never been to Boulder, CO, but have heard about all the great skiing in Colorado and want to relocate there to ski as much as possible, you must understand why a firm owner might be hesitant to hire you.

If you do relocate, plan to commit at least 36 months to your new position. Since financial planning is currently best learned under an apprenticeship model, there is something to be said about being in person, at least for a certain amount of time, when starting your career. It is much more difficult to observe, model, and practice when your interactions with your supervisors and colleagues are limited and only behind a screen or phone.

Element #5 — Fee Structure

Next, consider the firm's fee structure. How the firm is compensated is a deal breaker for many job seekers. You can find this information in the Firm's ADV Part 2 Brochures if they are a Registered Investment Advisor (RIA). If you can't pull an ADV, you must rely on the interview skills you are now prepared for. Explore the motivations behind the firm's decision and evaluate what matters to you. If there is no ADV and it is unclear on the website, you should ask your interviewer how their firm generates revenue.

Element #6 — Culture

The compensation you receive for your work is important, but a firm's culture is, arguably, just as or even more important. You don't want to arrive at a firm only to discover a toxic work environment or a culture in which you feel uncomfortable. One way to ensure you find a firm that fits you well is to identify cultural elements that matter to you. These are essential to your core values which should be on the non-negotiable side of the list you created.

Are you looking for a team-based firm? One that's innovative? Do you feel best in a growth-minded culture? Is a client-focused firm the place you feel most yourself? Do your best to ensure your values and standards align with the firm.

Element #7 — Growth

What about opportunities for growth? You want to grow professionally, right? Well, *your* professional growth is tied to the firm's growth. Be sure to ask clarifying questions about what it takes to be promoted and to take on increased responsibility. A stagnant firm can often indicate a firm reticent to offer swift advancement. You want to be in a firm that encourages growth in all areas and has the track record to back it up.

Element #8 — Mentorship

Earlier we talked about the importance of mentorship. Your mentors should be a loose representation of your future career goals. So, on the one hand, there's an intuitive nature to finding a good firm where mentorship is a strong element. You're looking for the type of advisor you'd like to be. And this can certainly be a "feel" thing.

On the other hand, you should also look to the credentialing and industry reputation of the advisors mentoring you. An advisor's credentials and reputation provide you with insight into whether they can speak to your career with gravitas and insight.

Remember, not all mentorships are created equal. To ensure you receive the deep and valuable mentorship you are seeking, clarify expectations behind the time devoted to helping you grow as an advisor and who will be responsible for taking the lead on the mentoring relationship.

Element #9 — Career Track

Identify the career track that fits your goals. Are you looking to be an employee who is paid a salary and serves other planners' clients? Are you entrepreneurial? Do you want to build your own business? Are you looking for a combination and more of a hybrid role? Ask yourself where you want to start and grow, then find the firms providing that opportunity.

Element #10 — Position

Entry-level positions in financial planning often go by many different names: paraplanner, associate advisor, associate financial planner, financial planning coordinator, financial planning associate, and the list goes on. There is no uniformity among the naming conventions, which is caused by the fact the profession has not been around very long and is entrepreneurial. Firm owners change the titles on a whim to match their career track and marketing materials and service offerings. This creates confusion and can be frustrating, but they are usually all the same position. As you are evaluating these roles, don't focus on the titles, but instead, identify the key responsibilities of the position and how they contribute towards your eventual goals.

Furthermore, determine what responsibilities you would like to do and ensure the firm has the structure to keep you focused on the responsibilities you most enjoy.

Element #11 — Administrative Tasks & Account Paperwork

Be prepared to roll up your sleeves and help with the administrative tasks that need to be done. Tasks such as answering the phone, copying paperwork, scheduling appointments, fixing computers, getting coffee, calling vendors, and ordering office supplies. While often overlooked, they are essential tasks to keeping the firm up and running and clients happy.

In a financial planning firm, paperwork is necessary for many tasks, from opening accounts to implementing various planning strategies.

For some, this is an insult; others love it. In whichever camp you find yourself in, you need to enter your new opportunity with a firm understanding that you will need to allocate time each day and week to stay on top of the administrative tasks that come with the job. Planning for this in your calendar makes it easier to schedule it. And scheduling it to ensure it gets done. Realize even at the highest level of firm management; there is still some level of admin work that those individuals do.

Element #12 — Client Meetings

Are you seeking involvement in client meetings? If so, what will be your role—Observer, note taker, partial presenter? If this is you, the hope is you've already garnered some experience in your internship. So, you should know what client meetings entail to hit the ground running.

Don't join a firm that doesn't offer you this opportunity if it's on your non-negotiable list. You will grow frustrated, affecting your production and, possibly, your reputation.

If you are not looking to be involved in client meetings, the other side of this coin applies to you. Don't put yourself in a position where the firm wants you to hold several client meetings daily. You don't want to be immediately stressed in a career path where you are doing things long-term that are not specific to your skill set and do not align with your goals.

Element #13 — Investment Operations & Financial Planning Analysis

I've joined these elements together because they relate well. And you need to understand how important they are to your routine tasks. Investment operations are opening accounts, transferring assets, including fund research, placing trades, and rebalancing client portfolios. You want to join a firm that has the software, systems, and people in place to have a solid back-office to help you serve the clients most effectively.

Placing trades and researching and rebalancing portfolios will become routine. However, the profession is moving towards more passive investing (not trying to beat the market) from active investing (trying to consistently outperform the market). More and more firms are fully outsourcing investment management functions to Turnkey Asset Management Platforms (TAMP) that take the investment activities mostly off a firm's plate so they can focus on the client relationship and add more value since they can devote more time to financial planning.

The area of financial planning analyses is the lifeblood of the firm. Clients are working with the firm for their advice and recommendations. If you don't give good advice, it doesn't matter how nice the clients think you are; they will quickly find another professional.

Will you input information into planning software, interpret the data, or specialize in a certain planning area?

What kind of research and resources will you have access to?

Ask these kinds of questions as you consider your employer. Entering a position and understanding your role and the important elements of your role puts you well ahead of the pack.

Element #14 — Business Development

Do you want to find new clients for your firm? If you are excited to build a book of business on your own, great. You will likely be able to get to where you want to go from a personal income standpoint faster than someone more comfortable in a long-term back-office type role where they are relying on someone else to develop the clients and generate the revenue. You might consider asking what marketing platforms and resources are available. For example, does the firm put on seminars, buy lists of names so you can make cold calls, and advertise on the radio, TV, or social media?

Element #15 — Non-Planning Efforts

You might have interests outside of financial planning advice delivery and client service that can be valuable to the firm, such as designing a new brochure, updating the website using your coding skills, or reading a new book to share with clients. Will you have the flexibility to explore, pursue, and use those interests to contribute to the firm?

***

Finding a good fit firm is not about finding a job.

When you set out to discover a firm, you are looking for an entire package. You could say "Yes!" to the first firm that shows interest in you, and it could end up being an awful fit. Have patience, and don't let FOMO interfere with your pre-established plan as I almost did.

Discovering your first place of employment is about matching your vision for your career with the firm that aligns with that vision. You want the relationship between you and your firm—your colleagues, bosses, and mentors—to be symbiotic. You don't want the firm you join to take and take and leave you so frustrated that you can't grow into new roles because you are so bogged down. You want the firm you join to see your hiring as a mutually beneficial relationship that helps you both get to where you want to go by investing in you. That's what I call a win-win.

Key Takeaways

- The sooner you can figure out where you want to be, the sooner you will get there.

- Finding a good fit firm takes time.

- Make sure you have spent time and effort in developing your position negotiables and non-negotiables.

- Develop goals that will get you to where you want to be.

- Ask lots of questions to help you determine firm, role, and future growth opportunity fit.

Action Items

- Review Chapter 6 Materials using this QR Code.

- Write down 1-2 short-term goals for yourself.

- Write down 1-2 mid-range goals for yourself.

- Write down 1-2 long-range goals for yourself.

CHAPTER 7

—·—

AVOID THESE JOB SEARCH KILLER MISTAKES

"It has long been an axiom of mine that the little things are infinitely the most important."
—Sir Arthur Conan Doyle

Success begins with, "Thank you." In our fast-paced me-first world, it's easy to fall into bad habits that communicate selfishness over service. When this happens, the fine details in professional life can get swept under the rug. But don't let this happen to you. Take care of the details because they matter.

If you want to show your new employer how prepared you are, then it's time to replace unfocused behavior with meaningful habits.

You don't want to mess up your first impression with potential employers by being ill-prepared. Many people fail to understand the importance of the little things in a job search. Getting an interview is only half of the journey.

In this chapter, I want to share some common mistakes that early-career financial planners make. You'll learn the value of paying attention to the little things that can set you apart from the pack.

Avoid These Common Mistakes

If you want the best possible chance at securing a great position, then start by noting these common mistakes you should avoid at all costs.

Saying only "Hello" when you answer the phone for a scheduled interview.

Don't do this. It's very unprofessional. In my experience, college students and Millennials are the biggest offenders. Think about it; you need to answer the phone the way you would when employed. Why not something like, "*Hello, this is John.*" or "*Good afternoon, Jane Smith is speaking.*" You will be expected (and required) to answer the phone this way in your job when representing a firm.

Not outdressing your interviewer.

Business professional is where you want to be. Solid colors and pinstripes are the best. Cotton shirt and silk tie, if possible, with black or brown shoes. The ladies should think of slacks with a jacket or skirt with a blouse. Think simple and conservative with jewelry and avoid showing too much skin. Gentlemen should avoid unkempt facial hair. If you aren't sure, trend on the more conservative side. It's always better for an interviewer to tell you to take off the tie, coat, etc., versus telling you that you should have worn one.

Failing to spend the appropriate amount of time researching the firm you've applied for.

This is a big one. And it's unacceptable. If you're "too busy" to look at a website, LinkedIn profile, Facebook page, Twitter feed, or whatever it may be, hiring firms are too busy to interview you.

If you can't spend a few hours preparing for an interview that could potentially land you a position paying $50k or more per year, then you need to revisit your time management skills. Take the time. Know your potential employer. It shows initiative, and that's a good thing.

Failing to call to confirm your interview.

Call or at least email the day before and say something like this, *"Hello, this is _____. I wanted to confirm my interview with _____ tomorrow at 3pm at [state location]. Does this time still work for [state name of the person you are interviewing with]?"*

Then make sure you arrive at least 15 minutes early. I learned this the hard way. Early in my career, when I was working for someone who was 50 years older than I was, I showed up for work at 7:55 am for a start time of 8 am, which did not go over well. I thought I was doing great, arriving 5 minutes early, but he pulled me aside and told me a story of when he was starting his career, he would arrive 1 hour ahead of time. Of course, I thought that was silly, but it did help me understand how different generations think about things such as timeliness, etc. It is possible you could be going to work for someone who has similar views, so it is best to ask them what their expectations are.

Two-page resumes with little to nothing on the second page.

When I see this, I assume you haven't proofread the document again after you converted it to a PDF. Furthermore, it sends the message that you are poor at details.

"We receive dozens of cover letters per year and I always seem to get one with another firm's name on it. I stop reading and they immediately go into the reject pile. If they are too busy and/or can't pay attention to the details, we can't have them at our firm working with our clients."

—Bruce J., Financial planning firm owner in California

Boilerplate cover letters.

We can tell when you cut and paste from another document, especially when you forget to make the font and style consistent. If you can't take a few moments to proofread your work, you aren't going to get a job with a top financial planning firm.

Blank email.

You attach your resume and send it via email, but don't put a title on the email or a message in the email. You are expecting someone else to figure out why you sent it and what you are looking for. How about titling something like this, "Caleb Brown Resume for Associate Planner Position at XYZ Firm" and in the body of your email:

Hello [FNAME],

It was terrific meeting you today at the conference. As promised, here is my resume. I also applied to your posting on your website, but I wanted you to have a copy as well. When would be a good time for us to talk again about how I can add value to your organization?

Sincerely,

[Your Name]

You can't articulate solid reasoning for choosing financial planning as a career.

You must set yourself apart from others by not only knowing why you want to be a financial advisor but articulating it well.

Everyone says it's because they want to work with numbers and help people. Show your passion for the industry! Get specific. Get creative. When you can explain your passion to a potential employer well, it conveys your enthusiasm for the career choice you've made.

Overdo it on the food and alcohol.

It is highly likely you will be having a meal with your potential employer as part of the interview process. Here are some guidelines on mastering the mealtimes:

- Order something easy to eat. Probably not a good idea to order a full rack of ribs, fried chicken, crawfish, or other messy foods.

- If in a more formal setting, work outside to in with the

silverware.

- Taste your food before seasoning. Covering your meal with salt and smothering it with butter without tasting is off-putting and, in some cultures and parts of the country, very offensive to the chef/meal preparer.

- Keep your hands in your lap and elbows off the table.

- Break bread and then butter, pass the butter and pass salad dressing.

- Strive to cut two to three bites of food at a time so you aren't looking downward cutting your food the entire meal.

- Don't talk with your mouthful, and don't drink while your mouth is full to wash your food down—no one wants to see or hear that. Wait until your bite is finished, then go in for a drink; it's also better for your digestion this way.

- Be yourself, but consider sticking to soft drinks, tea, and water for your beverage. Having a few drinks and lowering your inhibitions could cause you to put your foot in your mouth and blow the entire interview.

Do the Little Things Because They Matter

Don't shun the grunt work.

You need to get comfortable with the idea of paying your dues. Don't become the stereotype for people in your generation! Embrace the hard, boring work. Everyone in the profession had to start somewhere, and for most, that was the bottom. They worked their way up. Plus, it is a great way to learn. You must learn the basics.

Don't forget to send a thank you note after your interview.

If you fail to do this, you are saying, *"I'm not that interested in my career."* You're showing your lack of professionalism.

Sending a note to say thank you is a great way to follow up and show your passion and enthusiasm for the position. And go for it—write a handwritten note! This is the best route because it shows tremendous effort since very few people do it any longer. Buy some sharp stationery and put your best professional foot forward. But if you have illegible handwriting as I do, email is a solid second option.

Don't ask for time off right after starting your new job.

Do you want a guaranteed way to irk your co-workers and your supervisor? Then ask. But if you want to build up social capital—instead of burning it up before you even start—then get to work and serve your team before you leave them stranded. If you have something planned and you know it will fall on a date after you start, then tell the firm when you are discussing start dates.

Don't negotiate your salary via email.

We live in a digital world. And that's a blessing and a curse. There are some things in life that must be discussed in person, and this is one of them. It doesn't matter how eloquently you draft your email; a firm owner will take it the wrong way because a person's tone is harder to pick up in email versus face-to-face or via phone. Pick up the phone and call them. Thank them for the offer; then you can get clarification and start negotiations.

Don't place too much emphasis on your title.

As I mentioned earlier, the financial planning profession doesn't have consistent titles. Your title is probably going to be something like Financial Planning Associate, Associate Financial Planner, or Financial Planning Analyst, and some firms might even let you pick your own title. Don't fuss over it.

Don't wait for someone to tell you what to do.

You need to learn to take the initiative and understand that your professor, who may have provided a syllabus, grading rubric, and detailed instructions on each assignment, is no longer around. Avoid sitting around. Instead, take a swing and ask someone what you need to be doing if you aren't clear.

Never talk negatively about previous employers and team members.

Big no-no here. This is a major turnoff for firms. It is unprofessional. Your firm would think you would do the same thing to them if you left their organization. Keep any dirty laundry confidential.

But what if your new firm asks you why you are leaving your previous firm? You can say something as simple as, *"The direction of the firm has changed, and it was no longer a fit for me."* This will work most of the time. Some firms will push you to share more. If you must do so, try to do it in the most positive light you can.

Consider turning your social media profiles to private.

If hiring firms can find unflattering pictures or comments about you on the internet, so can their clients. This is very unprofessional and would reflect poorly on the firm. Remember, once you are hired, you reflect that organization in your community, in the profession, and on the internet. No one says you can't have fun; just turn it private so only your friends can see.

Don't boss existing staff on the first day—or ever.

You're confident. Great. That's an asset as a new planner. But you also need to learn to check your ego at the door. Telling someone what to do who has been at the firm longer than you have been alive will not work out well for you. Trust me. You have a shiny new degree in financial planning. Fantastic. Stick your degree on a wall at home or in your new office, and get to work.

You need to develop bonds with your co-workers because they are your key to success in a new position or in a new firm. The last thing a firm owner wants is for you to cause strife in what was a harmonious office environment.

Don't skimp on the little things. They will set you apart. Look, it's wonderful that you're excited to be entering the job market. The potential is unlimited, right? You're eager and can't wait to get going and find success.

But success begins by making your bed in the morning. It begins with saying thank you to the person who hands you your café mocha. Success begins with helping your new neighbor move some boxes. My point is success begins with all the little things that are easy to overlook because they don't *seem* to have any bearing on financial planning or your career.

Trust me when I say that all those little things—those acts of thoughtfulness and kindness—spill over into your professional life. If you're overly bossy at home, you'll be one at the office. If you're thoughtless in your communication with your friends and family, you'll communicate selfishness at the office.

Take all the "Don'ts" in this chapter and turn them around. Become a letter writer. Be articulate about your passion for your work. Be a servant to your co-workers. You get the idea. Remember. Success begins with "Thank you" and gratitude in general.

The Story of My First Job

After I decided I was going to take the CFP® Exam in July after I graduated in December, I planned to continue working for the insurance brokerage firm where my school was located while I studied for the exam. Then I would hopefully be able to start with a new firm shortly after passing the exam. My life was pretty simple at that point, and I threw everything I had into passing the test and finding a full-time job in a financial planning firm in the Dallas/Ft Worth, Texas area where I could start in August.

I utilized a very similar approach as I did when I secured the internship and part-time job (finding something that works and sticking with it!) of putting together packets to highlight my credentials and sending them to firms I had identified that I thought I would like to work for in the DFW area. I also contacted a financial planner in Dallas, Bryan Lee, who had visited my school as part of his duties as the FPA of DFW Chapter President and spoke to one of my classes. I told him I was looking in DFW and knew he had a lot of connections and asked him to keep his eye out for me, which he agreed to do. I hoped for a much quicker process and less rejection this time around, but alas, I was in for yet another surprise. The stock market still wasn't performing that well, and many firms were hesitant to hire someone young and unproven. After my mass mailing project, I was able to get a few firms to agree to a phone interview, but I wasn't sure they were the right fit.

Not knowing what to do, I reached out to Bryan and asked if he had any leads which he did not. I also discussed with him the struggles I was facing, the several interviews I had, and if he had any inside information about these firms that might be able to help me. After a few discussions with him, he shared that even though he had recently started his firm, he might want to hire an Associate Planner assuming he was able to bring in a few of the clients he was pursuing to ensure stability and viability of his new venture. In one of our conversations, he mentioned that he appreciated my persistence and asked if I would be interested in a position with him. I told him, yes, and thought I had the job.

Boy, was I in for another surprise! A few weeks later, I heard some classmates discussing that they were interviewing with the person that I thought I had already had the job with. I had a moment of sheer panic since I knew I couldn't compete, GPA-wise, with some of my classmates. Here I was again, the perpetual underdog, so I immediately went into action, trying to come up with ways that I could differentiate myself.

I reviewed the notes I had from my conversations with Bryan and remembered he said he used Naviplan financial planning software. I had limited exposure to it during my internship, but thought it might be my way in. It turns out, Naviplan was having a 2-day training session in Dallas, TX later that month. I knew I needed to go as I was confident that would make me stand out. Only one problem, the cost was $500 for the two days, which I didn't have at the time. It was also during the week, so I would have to miss work and school. I ended up putting $500 on my credit card, missing class, taking off work, and driving five hours to stay with a friend to attend the training.

I was the youngest person in training by at least twenty years. People were looking at me strangely; I was beginning to think I had made a big mistake, spending all that money, driving down, trying to learn a software program, and having no idea whether it would pay off or not. Turns out one of the people I was seated next to knew Bryan, whom I was interviewing with, and trying to impress, and word got back that I had attended the training and none of the other job candidates had. It ended up working out for me, and I got hired. My new boss later told me that I was not the best candidate, at least on paper, but I showed more initiative than anyone else, and he wanted someone like that on his team.

The goal that I had set for myself was to pass the CFP® exam and have at least one job offer. The firm in California said they would hire me, but I chose the Dallas firm, even though it was less money because I thought the career growth opportunity was better and it was closer to my family.

I essentially joined a start-up. My boss, Bryan, had started the firm just a few years prior and didn't have much in the way of clients, revenue, or profits. It also didn't help that he was thirty years old and I was only twenty-two. He took a chance on me, though, and I knew he was committed to me when he took out a personally guaranteed line of credit to pay me $2,000 per month to start as an employee.

I was young and single at the time, so it worked out for me, but the job I was going into was for me to try and establish processes and procedures, run the financial planning software, and try to manage most of the entire firm while Bryan spent time outside the office sourcing all of the clients. It worked for the most part; even though I made a lot of mistakes, I learned a ton in the process. We worked long hours; however, I believed in the mission and was proud of what we had built during my five years there.

Key Takeaways

- Some conscientiousness and common sense will go a long way in helping you avoid mistakes.

- You are being researched, monitored, and measured by the hiring organization from the moment you make contact.

- Exhibit gratitude and humility in your interactions with others.

- Doors will open for you if you meet people and expand your network.

Action Items

- Take inventory of your professional wardrobe. You need to have at least one business suit, and you don't need to break the bank. Check out Amazon and brick-and-mortar retailers for last year's items they are marking down.

- Set a goal to go out of your way to do at least one kind thing for someone each day.

CHAPTER 8

—·—

OFFER NEGOTIATION AND NEXT STEPS

"*A new job is like a blank book, and you are the author.*"
—Unknown

Well, you did it.

You have received a job offer(s), congratulations!

The big pressure is off. Now you need to step into a new phase of the job search process: *negotiating your offer.*

You're probably asking, "Should I negotiate? And if so, how?" It's a great question and an important one. Negotiating can be tricky because most financial planning firms want you to feel like you are compensated fairly, so you can be focused on serving clients and representing the firm well. But firm owners can also be very sensitive and can take negotiating to mean you are not grateful for the opportunity and the level of compensation they have initially laid out. So you must proceed with care.

Deciding to negotiate compensation should be based on your personal need and finding a fair compensation figure for your experience and credentials. Make sure you always thank any potential employer for making you an offer of employment to join their firm. Then approach any negotiation very delicately and respectfully.

Focus On Overall Compensation

I encourage job seekers to focus on their total compensation package even though the natural tendency is to hyper-focus on just the gross salary figure. Your total compensation is made up of many more elements than the cash component. Here are the primary areas:

- *Base Salary*—A base salary is your fixed annual pay excluding other benefits, commissions, or bonuses.

- *Incentive Compensation*—Additional cash compensation you can earn above and beyond your base salary. Some bonuses will be based on personal performance, firm metrics, or a combination of both.

- *Retirement Plan Match*—Any matching, non-discretionary, or profit-sharing contributions on your retirement plan.

- *Insurance Contribution*—Factor in the firm's contributions towards any group health, disability, or life insurance benefits.

- *Continuing Education Budget*—As an early-career financial planner, continuing education and industry networking outside of your firm is important. Whether you decide to attend a conference or pursue professional designations, this budget is important.

- *Paid Time Off*—Paid time off is important in creating your work-life balance. Other benefits can include the ability to work from home and schedule flexibility.

Keep in mind that, it typically costs firms another ~20% of whatever your total cash compensation is for all of your benefits. So if your base compensation is $50,000, the firm is probably investing at least $60,000, which is easy to forget since it does not hit your bank account.

Understand Future Earnings and Career Potential

Remember that your early-stage career jobs will shape your late-stage career trajectory. For example, taking a position in an aggressively growing firm to provide ample opportunities to learn your craft or joining a firm with equity ownership potential is much more beneficial to you in the long run than a few thousand extra dollars per year in salary another firm might be offering.

You might like the sound of the extra money, but if the firm is paying you more and lacks the mentoring, learning opportunities, or career growth, you are short-changing yourself in the long run.

Throughout my career working with hundreds of firms across the country, I have found the opportunities leading to the best long-term outcomes are those that provide mentorship and training, so put your emphasis here.

Negotiating Salary

You need to know what you are worth within a reasonable range, and if you aren't sure what the going rate for a planner is, you can find more information in the Chapter 8 Resource section. Generally, though, for an entry-level, meaning someone right out of school with little to no experience, financial planning position nationwide, you can expect base compensation to start in the $45,000–$65,000 range. If you understand your compensation and future trajectory at a firm and feel the compensation is below your market rate or is at a rate too low for you to accept, here are some tips on broaching the subject:

Pick two or three key negotiating points.

Some are easier to negotiate than others, depending on the additional costs that an employer may incur. Some common negotiation points in financial planning firms include:

- Salary or Bonus Potential

- Job Title

- Start Date

- Vacation/PTO

- Technology Allowance

- Relocation Expenses

- Remote/Virtual Work

- Training, Association Dues, or Continuing Education Allowance

Ask questions rather than make demands.

If you're uncomfortable negotiating, phrase the questions in a way that asks what accomplishments you would need to reach a certain compensation or be eligible for the benefits you're seeking. After you ask, be quiet. Being comfortable with silence will assist you tremendously in lots of areas of your life, career, and negotiations. Plus there is no need to continue talking to justify yourself. Be still and let them respond.

Always negotiate face to face or via phone call.

As I shared in the last chapter, when you are presented with an offer and review it, schedule a time with the hiring manager to ask questions about the offer face-to-face. It's fine to use email to schedule a time to discuss the offer.

When you meet, relax. Don't speak quickly and nervously. You want to convey yourself as calm, likable, and confident in your value.

Understand the going rate for your position and skill set.

Make your counteroffer around fair and reasonable terms. It is not effective, nor professional, to ask for well-above-market compensation with the intent of settling somewhere lower or in the middle.

Be prepared for them to say no.

If the compensation piece is that important to you, you need to be prepared to walk away if the offer doesn't meet your expectations or needs.

Be mindful of the social capital you use to negotiate an offer.

Remember, the firm has invested time, effort, and resources in you. By extending an offer, they are demonstrating their desire to make you part of their team. While most firms will not revoke their initial offer, keep in mind you will be working intimately with the same people you are negotiating with.

Get any changes in writing in the form of a new offer letter.

Here is a sample script for the phone call if you feel like you must negotiate your compensation.

...Thank you so much for the offer! I am very excited about the opportunity and had a few questions and wanted to go over a few things.

I didn't see when I would be eligible for the 401k and health insurance plans. Is there a waiting period on those?

I really appreciate you covering the CFP® materials and exam fee. How does that work? Do I pay then get reimbursed?

I talked to my professors and some other colleagues who received offers for the same position at similar firms and have reviewed all the industry salary surveys and the consensus was this is a fair offer. However, I would like to be in the top quartile for cash compensation/salary vs. the average.

What do I need to be able to do/learn or bring to the table to help the firm to start at $_____ versus $_____?

You want the best deal for yourself, but remember, if you choose the right firm, the mentoring, coaching, and experience, you shouldn't have too much trouble earning a living. Getting started in the right firm with the right people and mentors is worth a lot more than a few thousand dollars per year, that another opportunity might pay you in the short term.

As with everything in life, honesty is the best policy, so if you do have another offer, it is fine to bring it up. Realize, however, that firm owners are very wary and can get agitated if they feel like you are using one offer to leverage something else out of them.

If you run into this, assuming you do have a legit additional offer, you can say something like this on the call:

"I have an offer for $_____ at another firm. I think I am a better fit for your firm though. Can you match it?"

You should always be prepared for them to say no.

Examples of Offers, Successful and Unsuccessful Negotiations
Offers accepted with little to no negotiation

New college graduate — $500MM–$1 Billion AUM Midwest fee-only RIA offered $55,000 base salary plus 10% bonus, 3 % 401k match, cell phone reimbursement, $400/mo. towards medical insurance, 2 weeks vacation.

Recent college graduate with one yr. of experience — $500MM–$1 Billion AUM Midwest fee-only RIA offered $58,000 base salary, 10% bonus, 3% 401k match, CFP® renewal fee covered, $1,000 training and conference budget, two weeks vacation.

New college graduate — $100MM–$250MM AUM Midwest Hybrid RIA offered $45,000 base salary, 10% incentive, SIMPLE 3% match, $2,500 bonus for passing licensing exams, two weeks vacation.

New college graduate — $100MM–$250MM AUM Midwest Hybrid RIA offered $50,000 base salary, three weeks vacation, CFP® renewal fee, CFP® program tuition reimbursement up to $7,000.

New College graduate — $500MM–$1 Billion AUM East Coast fee-only RIA offered $47,000, plus $5,000 signing/relocation bonus, business development bonus of 30 basis points for any new AUM brought in, health, retirement, and unlimited PTO.

Recent college graduate with six months of experience — +1 Billion AUM Midwest fee-only RIA offered $60,000 base salary, 10% bonus, 3% 401k match, CFP renewal fee, $1,000 training and conference budget, two weeks vacation.

New college graduate — $250MM–$500MM AUM Southeastern fee-only RIA offered $57,000 base salary, 100% employer-paid health coverage, 30% of the first-year fee for new client sourcing bonus, annual discretionary bonus and net new revenue quarterly bonus, 3% 401k match, 2 weeks vacation.

New college graduate — $250MM–$500MM AUM Southeastern fee-only RIA offered $50,000 base salary, $2,500 increase once licensing exams passed, SIMPLE IRA plan, unlimited PTO, health and wellness $50 mo., $100 mo. phone and internet reimbursement, one month paid sabbatical every five years of service.

Career Changer with three years of experience — $250MM–$500MM AUM Southeastern fee-only RIA affiliated with an accounting firm offered $70,000 plus a $2,000 signing bonus, plus annual discretionary bonuses, 401k, and health insurance plan with 100% of premiums covered for new hire.

New college graduate — $100MM–$250MM AUM Mountain West fee-only RIA offered $48,000, increasing to $60,000 once licensing exams passed, 10% incentive bonus, four weeks PTO, 4% 401k match.

<u>Recent college graduate</u> — $500MM–$1 Billion AUM Southeastern hybrid RIA offered $65,000, plus $5,000 bonus for passing CFP® exam, 401k plan, health insurance premiums paid 50% by hiring firm.

<u>Career Changer</u> — $250MM–$500MM AUM Northeastern fee-only RIA offered $67,500, plus incentive, company cell phone, 401k, and health insurance plan.

<u>New college graduate</u> — $100MM–$250MM AUM Southeastern hybrid RIA offered $60,000, $5,000 bonus once CFP® exam passed, salary increases to $65,000 once CFP® credential can be used, 4% quarterly bonus paid on new insurance revenue, six basis points for net new assets bonus.

<u>CFP® with eight years of experience</u> — $250MM–$500MM AUM Mountain States fee-only RIA offered $100,000 plus a 15% target bonus, 401k, and health, dental and disability insurance plan with 100% of premiums covered.

<u>Recent College Graduate with one year of experience</u>—$100MM–$250MM AUM fee -based Mid-Atlantic RIA offered $60,000 plus $5,000 bonus for passing Series 65, increasing salary to $70,000 when able to use CFP® credential.

Examples where negotiating did not work

<u>New college graduate</u> — $500MM–$1 Billion AUM Northeast fee-only RIA offered $52,000 base salary, countered with $62,000 and the firm rejected and rescinded the offer.

<u>Recent college graduate with one year of experience</u> — +$1 Billion AUM West Coast fee-only RIA offered $57,000 base salary, countered with $65,000 and the firm rejected, candidate ended up joining firm anyway.

<u>Career changer with no experience</u> — $100MM–$250MM AUM Southwest fee-only RIA offered $60,000, countered with $65,000 and unlimited PTO, and the firm rejected.

Examples where negotiating did work

Career Changer — $250MM–$500MM AUM Northwest fee-only RIA offered up to $400 monthly insurance stipend for individual coverage and asked for the entire family to be covered by the employer, $750 month the employer granted.

New college graduate — $100MM–$250MM AUM Northeast hybrid RIA offered $55,000 base salary and countered with $57,000, agreed upon by the employer.

Recent college graduate with six months experience — $100MM–$250MM AUM Mid-Atlantic fee-only RIA offered two weeks vacation/PTO countered with unlimited which was granted by employer and rolled out to existing team members.

Employee Benefit Packages

In addition to a base salary, bonus/incentive compensation, you should also expect to receive some type of retirement and health insurance plan at a minimum. On the other side of the spectrum, firms might offer paid financial planning so you and your significant other can go through the planning process, paid sabbaticals, unlimited PTO, commuting allowances, gym memberships, professional sports tickets, etc. I've included a chart below to give you a better feel for what type and level of benefits are available to you.

	Retirement	Health Insurance	Vacation/PTO	Tech	Financial Planning	Training	Education
Table Stakes	401k with employer match	Group Plan available	2 weeks	Basic tech: PC, dual monitors, phone, wireless headset	Initial allocation and ongoing management of company retirement account	$1,000/yr.	Reimburse for successful passage of CFP® exam; $595
Better	401k with match & profit sharing	Employer subsidizes at least 50% of premium of group plan	2 weeks–4 weeks	Upgraded tech: think iMac, MacBook Pro, Surface Pro; cell phone mo. reimbursement	New hire and spouse/partner go through initial planning process, ongoing investment management	$1,000–$3,000/yr.	CFP® coursework, CFP® exam review and CFP® exam cost; > $3,000
Best	Roth 401k w PSP	100% employer paid premiums for covered employee and dependents	Unlimited, 1 month paid sabbatical after 5 yrs of service	Replace PC every 2 years or as needed plus high speed internet and cell phone mo. reimbursement	1st year fee covered for new hire and spouse/partner for financial planning and investment mgmt via another trusted firm	$3,000–negotiable/yr.	Advanced education (MBA, MSFS, etc.) and credentialing (CPWA, CFA, etc.) that could reach as high as $50k or more total

Keep in mind as well that with most small financial planning firms, whatever you are paid comes directly from what the firm owner takes home to their family so asking for more isn't an issue in itself but it is helpful to have a perspective from the other side of the negotiation table.

It is worth noting most employers will require you to pass a background, credit, and sometimes a drug screening test, so be prepared for these. If you know you have something on the background or credit, it is better to tell the employer upfront so they can determine the best course of action before getting through the process and becoming frustrated and probably rescinding your offer. A good interviewer will probably ask you in the very first interview if there is anything on your background check that might show up.

You also may be asked to sign a non-compete, non-solicit, and non-disclosure as part of your employment. Here is an overview of each of those documents and what it means to you:

Non-Compete

This agreement states that if you leave the firm, you will not join a competitor or start your firm for a certain time and certain proximity to your previous firm. This agreement protects the employer from departing employees who might negatively impact their business. How would an ex-employee do this?

Imagine after a few years working for a company, learning everything about their business, someone takes that knowledge to a competitor or starts their own business. Consideration, above and beyond base salary, must be received in conjunction with you signing this for it to be enforceable. Enforceability must also be reasonable for a judge to uphold it.

For example, if a firm tries to get you to sign a non-compete that says something like, " … *won't compete for five years within a 100-mile radius*" the judge is likely to toss that out due to the fact that *'an employer can't completely keep someone from earning an income.'*

Keep in mind non-compete agreements vary from state to state. So, make sure you understand the guidelines of enforcement in your state of employment.

Non-Solicitation

This agreement states that if you leave the firm, you will not directly or indirectly contact the prior firm's client/customer list to try and get them to join your new organization. This mostly applies to clients that are given to you by the firm. If you bring in any clients directly yourself, usually the non-solicitation does not apply to those clients.

Now, in all reality, clients can go wherever they want. If they do decide to follow you to a new firm, there isn't a whole lot the prior firm can do. Especially if you can prove that you did not reach out to them and instead, they sought you out and found you at the new firm.

In this case, most firms come up with a buyout provision such as, *"You will be required to pay 1x annual revenue for each client that follows you."* Even with these provisions, the likelihood of potential litigation is high if the clients in question are larger and generate substantial amounts of revenue.

Non-Disclosure

This agreement states that if you leave the firm, you will not share any trade secrets and/or other confidential materials with another competitor firm.

It is all fair and reasonable for firms to have you sign these agreements if they give you time to review them and do not put them in front of you and require you to sign without reviewing first.

So, be prepared. Also, consider hiring an attorney and paying a few hundred dollars to have the agreements reviewed to make sure you know what you agree to. It is also fine to tell the potential employer you need a few days to have the documents reviewed.

***

Well, you've navigated the negotiation of your compensation. You're ready to hit the ground running. What can you do between accepting the offer and your first day?

I've come up with a few things you can do between any elapsed time from accepting an offer and starting your new job. In certain situations, you could accept a position but not start for a few weeks, months, or in some rare cases, even years. You can sit on the couch and revel in your job search success. Or you can maximize the time. Can you guess what I'd suggest you'd do?

Here's a list of guidelines on maximizing the time in between when you sign on the dotted line and when you walk into your new office.

1. Tell your family, friends, and professors about your new gig! Don't be surprised if a few people say they want to work with you and your new firm.

Here is an example of something you could say:

'Hello Everyone,

I hope you are doing well. I wanted to update you on my career since graduating from [insert school's name]. After months of researching, soul-searching, and interviewing, I have accepted an offer to start as an Associate Financial Planner with [insert company name], a very reputable financial planning firm that matches my core values and has a long history of helping people achieve their goals.

I am very excited to begin my career as a financial planner and work with a team that puts their client's needs ahead of their own and is committed to me and my career. I would like to talk with you more about this opportunity and what I am doing in my new role at the firm. You can see my bio page here [insert a link to bio page]

Again, I would love to catch up with you when you have a moment. You can reach me at [insert phone number] and [insert company email address].

Best,

[Newly Hired New Planner]

2. Complete all the onboarding paperwork required by the firm. Here is a sample list:

- Passport or ID card with photo

- W4

- I9

- Direct deposit

3. Obtain housing if relocation is involved. Some firms might have relationships with realtors, access to corporate apartments, potential roommates, sub-leases, or subsidized housing.

4. Ask to be copied on pertinent company emails—this will help you understand the communication flow within the firm and better position you to hit the ground running.

5. Ask for early access to software systems—Observe who is doing what by when. This will give you a feel for how the organization utilizes technology.

6. Start learning the clients' backstories that you will be working on. If you can obtain access to the CRM software, you should be able to review the client history. New planners who show up on the first day and already show some familiarity with the clients will blow their employers away.

7. Download all the user manuals for the software programs and any other tools the firm employs. At least try to skim through these but reviewing video tutorials is ideal.

8. Take a few days or a few weeks, if you are able, to rest, relax and recharge before starting to ensure you can have a strong start because it may be a while before you can take significant time off again.

Some firms may not want to provide you early access to systems, software, client data, and the like. But the top candidates will ask for this because they know that the more prepared they are for their first day, the better off everyone will be.

Don't approach this little list feeling overly pressured. Enjoy your prep time. Stay relaxed but focused. Now is a great time to start implementing good personal habits that will infuse your first day and week of work with enjoyment and vigor. And what about that first day? It's a big deal, right? First impressions and all that. Well, keep reading, my friend.

Key Takeaways

- Salary is only one small part of your compensation package.

- Seek out the positions where you will learn the most, not necessarily the one that pays you the most.

- Your first day is a momentous occasion for you—prepare for it so it will be memorable and remarkable.

- Make sure you are comfortable with the language in the non-compete, non-solicit, and non-disclosure before signing.

- In any good negotiation, both parties feel like they are giving something up.

Action Items

- Review Chapter 8 Materials using this QR Code.

- List what employee benefits you would like to have versus what you must have.

- Send your family and friends a communication announcing your new position.

- Consider hiring an attorney or a trusted advisor to review any legal documents, such as a non-compete associated with your hiring.

CHAPTER 9

—·—

TRANSITIONING FROM STUDENT TO PROFESSIONAL

"It takes courage to grow up and become who you truly are."
—E.E. Cummings

Completing your CFP® certification coursework for entrance into the financial planning profession is an exhilarating time in your life, so make sure you take the time to celebrate it. Don't underestimate the gravity of what you are about to encounter. Making the transition from a student to your first job in your new career can be challenging. You might have to move to a different geographical area. You will have to learn the personalities of your new co-workers and the processes and procedures of your new firm. You will also have to learn all the client situations you'll be serving going forward.

The new planners who make this transition successfully are those who can adapt and adjust to a professional environment. That means a faster pace, less direction, and higher expectations from your direct supervisor and co-workers.

Here's a glimpse of what you will need to commit yourself to and what you can expect. A bit challenging but also exhilarating:

- Learn and contribute to the overall success of the organization.

- Get ready to move (geographically!), or learn from afar by watching videos.

- Get used to adopting a new schedule.

- Throw yourself into learning new software, processes, and procedures.

- Get to learn the personalities of your new co-workers.

- Commit to learning the individual situations of the clients your firm serves.

- Expect less direction from supervisors.

- Gear up for more critical thinking and problem-solving.

- And you might be studying for the CFP® exam on top of all of this!

But don't let this list intimidate you. This is what you signed up for. Use it as an incentive to get ready for what is sure to be a great adventure in your career.

Pathway and Timing

As you approach your graduation date, it is an exciting time in your life that you need to enjoy, but keep in mind there are lots of moving parts. You can refer back to the Internship and Job Search Pathway and Timing resource introduced in Chapter 4 to help guide you with the timing of some of the major decisions you will have to make to ensure your career is on track.

It's no secret that I am an advocate of the next generation of financial planners and consistently rebuff the efforts of those who try to stereotype all the 150 million members that make up Generation Y (Millennials) and Generation Z as lazy, arrogant, entitled, and overall just bad.

I am realistic, though, and in speaking to thousands of candidates from these generations thus far in my career and seeing some struggle in firms (even though many more succeed), I will acknowledge that there are a few out there who do not shed such a positive light on the rest! There is still room for some Millennial and Generation Z advisors to step up regarding their basic professionalism.

So, I've created this guide for the next generation of contributors to the financial planning profession. My hope is it will provide you with steps you can take to help you improve.

The Next Generation Team Member Pledge

I will observe and monitor how others in my organization are dressed and always dress at that level and/or strive for a higher level.

Insight: As we mentioned in Chapter 4. If you are the new hire and everyone else wears a long sleeve shirt and slacks, you should target that, plus a tie. This applies to clients as well. No one should out-dress you. After you have proven yourself, as Mark Zuckerberg has, then you can call your shots and consider dressing like him.

I will be at my desk ready to work and available to clients at the specified time.

Insight: If work hours at your firm are 8–5 p.m., show up half an hour early to get your chit-chatting done before you need to be fully engaged for your clients and other team members.

Additionally, everyone usually cannot take a lunch break at the same time, so be flexible and offer to go whenever no one else wants to. You might not think so, but someone is keeping a mental record of this, and your team-supporting deeds will build a favorable balance in your "trust bank" with those you work with.

I will not let my cell phone become a distraction.

Insight: Respect your employer's time and work at least for the time they are paying you. Understand that you are in a service business, and you might have to work longer to take care of the clients who are your ultimate boss. In most cases, you are being paid for the end results, not the time/hours worked. Even if you are worried about missing something, incessantly checking your phone will only make it worse. I heard from a firm owner one time who had recently conducted a multi-day interview, spending significant time over meals, at the office, in transit, etc., with a candidate, and one of the things that stood out to them was that they never saw the job seeker pull out their phone. It may sound silly, but employers are looking this closely at you!

I will watch my use of slang, industry jargon, and profanity.

Insight: Slang makes you come across as unintelligent, and industry jargon confuses your clients. And there is very little, if any, need for profanity. It does not matter how well you know the person, be careful going here and, frankly, you should probably just avoid this altogether while in work situations with clients, strategic alliances, and colleagues.

I will treat the members of my organization who are of the opposite gender with special respect.

Insight: Keep in mind this is not a weekend party. If you are looking for romance, it is likely going to work out better for all involved if you find it outside of your organization.

I will not expect my employer to make special exceptions for me due to a change in my personal and financial situation.

Insight: Realize any change in the relationship and/or financial status is not your employer's issue. It is your job to figure out how to live on a budget, if necessary, the same way you instruct your clients.

I will maintain a positive attitude and not complain.

Insight: If you are just starting your financial planning career, you are probably not adding much value in terms of revenue, AUM, profit, or any of the financial metrics that firm owners value. Someone is teaching you the business, letting you work on their clients, and paying you wages as well. This is infinitely more than what a lot of other people had when they entered the profession. Stay in gratitude!

"Gratitude unexpressed is ingratitude perceived."

—Lee Brower, Famed entrepreneur and coach of entrepreneurs

I will not be disruptive to my fellow office mates.

Insight: Your cube pals have a lot of work to get done as well. Be aware that your loud music, food and drinks, and chewing and smacking gum might be a distraction for them. Be thoughtful of how your daily routine affects those working near you.

I will communicate with my team if I am unable to come to work or do my job.

Insight: Always inform people who are relying on you if they can't rely on you or expect you for something. Call, email, or at least text as a professional courtesy. Don't ghost your team and supervisor or expect them to "figure out" what is going on with you.

I know that I am not likely my boss's #1 priority at all times.

Insight: Firm owners are under a lot of stress and pressure, which you do not see most of the time plus they have lots of other people to mentor as well.

I will treat clients as if they were family members that I like.

Insight: To give the best advice and have the deepest relationship, you have to like the clients even if they are not very likeable. Treat them how they want to be treated.

***

Furthermore, be diligent about your behavior at industry conferences because the financial planning profession is small, and word travels fast.

Here are some tips on how to handle yourself while at a conference and/or representing your firm in public:

1. Look your new contact in the eye, give a firm handshake, and state your full name. This will help them remember you.

2. Hold your drinks in your left hand to keep your right hand free for handshakes.

3. Strive to stand each time you are introduced to someone if you are seated.

4. Avoid controversial topics such as politics and religion. People are so easily offended these days; get to know them, get the job then you can more fully engage in these types of sensitive conversations.

5. Don't be tempted to look elsewhere when having a conversation. Maintain eye contact because it doesn't look good when you are looking around the room to see if someone else is more important.

Memo from Your Future Boss

Financial planning firms are constantly under pressure to do more with less to keep up with client demands, industry developments, and economic circumstances. This requires top performance from everyone in the firm, especially newbie hires.

Sometimes, this can be a difficult feat due to the unfortunate combination of unclear expectations, lack of structured training, and limited formal mentoring. When this happens, the relationship is strained, leaving the employee confused and the employer frustrated.

To help alleviate some of this tension, new planners should be aware of these four commonly cited *irks* by firm owners and take the necessary steps to avoid them. Following these, I've provided some tips for your first client meeting.

Irk No.1 — Lack of Initiative

Once you walk across the stage to receive your diploma, say goodbye to the days of rote memorization, regurgitation, and being spoon-fed all information needed for problem-solving. Firm owners become easily frustrated with new employees who cannot think critically and develop and defend a solution. I often get asked why new college grads wait for their employers to tell them exactly what to do. Among other things, I tell employers that it stems from the fear of making a mistake. And that fear comes from improper training and unclear expectations.

I polled some New Planner Recruiting clients on this very topic. Their responses confirmed what I surmised: *most firm owners would prefer you take a swing and miss versus not taking a swing at all.*

What's the takeaway?

A good manager will set up situations for you to take a swing that won't adversely impact the firm if you strike out. However, not everyone is a good manager. So, if that's the case in your situation, try asking your firm owner, *"Do I have your permission to run with this fully? If so, here is the direction I was thinking about. Do you have any other suggestions?"*

Irk No.2 — Unclear Passion

Firm owners want to see tangible signs that you are committed to the financial planning profession. They want to know that you are not merely trying it out on their dime because it looks fun. It takes work and commitment.

Realize financial planning is a difficult career, and you will experience hardship at some point during your career. Employers are looking for employees who will overcome and learn from these hardships and not let them keep them from what they love.

You must ask yourself, "Am I the type of financial planner who goes through the motions to have a job and live. Or am I the type of employee who lives to do financial planning?" There is a vast difference.

What's the takeaway?

Passion for your vocation cannot be taught. You either have it or you don't. You shouldn't spend your life doing something that doesn't fire you up.

Irk No. 3 — Repeating Mistakes

Due to the limited time that firm owners think they can devote to employee training and development, they may only be able to show you how to do something once or twice. This may be your only opportunity to learn, so take copious notes, ask questions, create screenshots, and practice a few times on your own if able.

Understand that you will probably have limited time with your firm owner. So, strive to maximize it by asking as many questions as it takes for you to be clear on their expectations before telling them you got it.

Keep a list of questions to review during your specified meeting times and refrain from asking dozens of one-off questions throughout the day, creating unnecessary interruptions.

What's the takeaway?

Avoid taking shortcuts and trying to do it "your way" until you have mastered *their* way. It is helpful to remember you were hired to take the pressure off the firm owner and existing staff to make their lives easier, not more difficult. The last thing you want to do is to create more work and stress.

Irk No.4 — Thinking Like an Employee

This is a tough one because technically, you are an employee! A lot of times, successful team members have a "think like an owner" mentality from day one. Employees are focused on getting *their* work done. Owners, however, are focused on getting *the* work done to wow their clients.

To get to that point, consider how what you are doing affects the client, the process, or firm overall instead of focusing on getting tasks crossed off your list. This also means owning up to mistakes you have made or think you have made.

Lofty expectations aside, firm owners understand mistakes will happen, so the best thing you can do is to own up to them. Waiting until the last minute to let someone know that you have not completed a project and will miss the deadline drives employers crazy. Don't be nervous about letting your supervisor know you cannot get something done. Consider asking them what their top priority is if you struggle to prioritize long task lists so you have a baseline expectation.

What's the takeaway?

Take responsibility for projects and complete your work as if it is the final, client-ready version. Do not assume someone else will do a final review to catch errors. When a project or plan gets to your firm owner's desk, there should be very few adjustments required. Once you can do this, you are bringing significant value to the firm because it gives your supervisors confidence in your work so they can give you more things to work on which frees up their time to focus on other things.

Remember, no matter how poorly you think your boss communicates and manages, keep a positive attitude and take the initiative by thinking like an *owner*. If you do these things, your passion will show, and you might be surprised how receptive your boss will be.

How to Wow Your Boss: Tips for Your First Client Meeting

So, now you know what not to do to irk your boss. But what about some insight into showing your boss you're on top of things?

If you want to *wow* your boss, you will want to crush it in your first client meeting. The following tips will set you up for success. But it's up to you to see them through.

Set an agenda for your meetings.

Sticking to an agenda will help you stay focused and accomplish what both you and the client expected to accomplish. It is even more helpful to send the client the agenda a few days before the meeting. Sending the agenda not only helps you think ahead but also helps manage client expectations for the meeting.

Ask open-ended questions.

This method not only helps clients to feel heard, but it also helps them to process their thoughts while providing you with helpful information. Clients are more likely to share information when they feel you are listening than if you are trying to get answers from them as they were going through an interrogation.

Take notes.

Taking notes is what I like to call active listening. Your notes also help you document and categorize information for yourself should meetings and clients start to run together in your mind. Note-taking makes clients feel as though you are taking what they have to say seriously. However, be careful not to appear too distracted by attempting to write every word.

Pay attention to body language.

Body language is a clear indicator that someone feels comfortable or uncomfortable with you. You may need to use a different tactic or rephrase your questions to help clients have a more positive experience. People mirror others. If you would like to make someone feel more comfortable, consider your body language as well.

Don't assume your goals are their goals.

Be careful not to impose your dreams and wishes on the client. You need to help them develop their goals and give guidance on what is reasonable. You need to help them see what is possible. Not only will defining retirement goals help you plan with the client on a practical level, but it also helps clients to communicate where they see themselves in the future. This is an important piece of information to understand whether you need to do an expectation check. You can help the client understand how they can adjust their goals accordingly to help them have a more satisfying experience with your continued advice.

Treat each meeting with the same zest as if it's the first one.

This is a great practice. It allows clients to share additional information that they may have forgotten or did not feel comfortable sharing in the first few meetings. It safeguards you from making assumptions while helping the client feel understood. Finally, it helps you assess your client's needs with precision and reevaluate new angles of their plan and the next best step.

Key Takeaways

- The stakes are high when you are handling someone's financial affairs.

- Understand your boss has expectations that they do not always communicate clearly.

- Be in a constant state of learning and gratitude.

- Work hard to deliver in the areas that you control.

- Ask your supervisor how you are doing and what you can do to improve.

Action Items

- Read through the pledge a few times, take a picture of it, and save it somewhere for future reference.

- Practice taking notes by writing with your head up so you can maintain some level of eye contact.

CHAPTER 10

—·—

90 DAYS INTO YOUR FINANCIAL PLANNING CAREER

> "*A mind that is stretched by new experiences can never go back to its old dimensions.*"
> —*Oliver Wendell Holmes, Jr.*

Starting your career and a new job can be daunting. Maybe you took a full course load in college and worked part-time but were never required to log eight-to-twelve-hour days, day after day, with someone watching closely.

For a new financial planner, starting a career will require preparation and some lifestyle changes. Arming yourself with knowledge may give you an advantage over your peers.

Here's a bit of insight from a few planners who recently went through this to keep in mind as you begin this new journey:

"The first 90 days will feel a lot like drinking from a fire hydrant. Keep it at the front of your mind; you're there to learn, and learning is done through attentive listening and observation. Your desire to be like a sponge is an admirable trait. It is easy to feel like you're asking too many questions, but at the end of the day, this industry is filled with passionate people, and passionate people love to teach."

—Luke S., CFP® joined RIA firm

"I had a lot of different emotions, anxiety, excitement, fear of the unknown going on. Plus there is so much to learn, and the schedule takes some getting used to. I have loved every minute of it though. It has been a wonderful experience."

—Sally J., ChFC® joined insurance company

In this chapter, I provide you with tips to help you navigate this life change successfully and an insider's insight into what to expect during your first 90 days on the job.

Setting Yourself Up for Success

First, the set up. An easy way to get started is to ask your manager how to prepare for your new role and ensure you know what metrics by which your manager defines success. *Establish a routine and solid habits early on.* Set aside time at the beginning of each day to ensure your physical, spiritual, and mental capacities are all in harmony. For some, this could be meditation, working out, reading, listening to music on your commute, and thinking. Consider starting the day off with a positive focus exercise where you think of 3–5 things you are thankful for before you start your day. You must focus on self-care too.

Also, spend a few minutes each morning writing down what you want to accomplish that day. Make sure to notate the time slot you will work on it, how long you estimate it will take, and the priority level you set for it. For example, you might set your "Client meeting prep" as your priority because it is something you absolutely must get done. Your second priority might be checking the status of the Smith account transfer status.

Be aware of the types of tasks you give yourself in the morning and afternoon. If you are a morning person (meaning you do your best work then), you want to strive to complete all your heavy thinking work in the morning and save your less intensive thinking tasks for the afternoon.

Likewise, if you hit your cognitive stride in the afternoon, get your emails, follow-ups, less intensive things done in the morning to free you up in the afternoon when you do your best thinking. People are wired differently, and no one does their best thinking all of the time.

Find your groove and do the best you can to set up your day around it if possible. Also, keep in mind the routine you had as a student may not work quite as well in your professional career setting. So, be prepared to adjust.

Finally, make a strong first impression and consider bringing your new coworkers gifts ($5 Starbucks gift card) or something to help you get started on the right foot with them. Most of the time, they are one of your biggest drivers to success. Celebrate your wins and success but give your team the credit. Hard to do, yes, but vital to building solid rapport and establishing long-term success.

Make it a habit at the end of each day to go around and ask your supervisors if there is anything you can do before you leave for the day. They might not have anything, but they also might have something for you. This is a great way to build trust and show them you are a team player and not 100% focused on you and going home at 5 pm, but willing to pitch in and help when needed.

The First Month

Now that you're set up for success, what can you expect in your first month?

The first month will include meeting the team and learning the personalities, reviewing the clients, and learning the workflow of the office. You'll know within 30 days if the firm is a good long-term fit. The top employers know that they have about 30 days to *wow* you. Likewise, you have about 30 days or less to wow them.

Here are a few tips for getting your first month started well.

How To Avoid Feeling Overwhelmed

Start by asking your boss specific questions about their expectations. Use those expectations to create a 30–60–90–days plan, and make sure you communicate regularly about your progress. Managers won't know how you feel if you don't tell them. They are probably assuming you are fine unless they hear from you otherwise.

Organize your workspace by making full use of calendars, tools such as Workflowy, Evernote, and customer relationship management (CRM) software. Try to learn about your clients a handful at a time versus all at once, where it is easy to become quickly deflated. Track and celebrate your achievements, however small, to stay motivated.

Common Mistakes New Hires Make

Avoid wasting time on the Internet; you need to assume that everything you click on is being monitored and getting sucked into office politics or gossip. Make every effort to stay present and give your full attention to meetings, staff lunches, and social events. Take advantage of all available opportunities for networking with your co-workers.

Another area new hires struggle with is overconfidence, fear of asking questions, or simply not asking the right ones. Don't be too proud to ask questions if you don't know something. Research shows people who ask for advice are perceived as more competent than others who don't. Never assume or provide the wrong information, especially to clients. Your boss and co-workers will not think any less of you by asking questions, but they will think less of you if you let the clients down by missing a deadline or blurting out something that is blatantly wrong.

The first month is as important as ever to pay exquisite attention to details and the quality of your work. Always make sure your work is accurate and thorough. Review everything and double or triple-check for spelling or grammatical errors.

The Second Month

I love this quote by an RIA firm owner in California, about his advice for new planners for the first weeks on the new job:

"Expect to see many things you think don't make sense and need improvement. If you don't see them, you're not looking. Getting good at spotting potential issues and opportunities for improvement is essential to becoming a good financial planner. But beware of your initial impressions. Many of them will be correct, but an equal number probably won't be. And the only way you're going to learn which is which, is by asking thoughtful questions."

Great advice!

Here is another perspective from a supervisor in a wirehouse firm in Texas:

"We are going to throw a lot at you, and it may be overwhelming. It is imperative that you listen and think critically during this initial process because everything builds on it."

By your second month, you should begin to develop a better feel for your firm's workflow. That includes feeling more comfortable with their software. You'll continue learning about the clients, and you'll have the opportunity to see how senior planners handle each client differently. Most importantly, you'll begin gaining an understanding of the art vs. science of financial planning. Art means there is no real right way to do it, and science means there is a consistent standard for the right way to do something or the right advice to dispense in a certain situation.

Learning the art and science of financial planning takes time. But there are several ways you can get ahead. This includes role playing, working on case studies with co-workers, sitting in on client meetings, and any situations where you can observe client communications.

It's also helpful to read and study as much as you can about behavioral finance—which examines why and how people make decisions, especially around money. Taking it a step further, you may want to enroll in psychology, counseling, or communications classes, if you have not had them, to develop further these skills. Consider a Massive Open Online Course (MOOC) like this one via Coursera offered by Duke University. https://www.coursera.org/learn/duke-behavioral-finance

The Third Month

By your third month, you can expect to start feeling more confident in your role. You'll have learned most of the clients' needs. You'll be ready to start taking on more responsibilities, which can put you in the good graces of the senior planners. As you start feeling more at ease in your new role, incorporate these five bits of insight for taking your new job to the next level.

1 — Add Value to Your Organization

Among these responsibilities is adding value in the technology and software area. A firm's software suite is an integral tool for financial planners, so it's important to get to know it well. Watching tutorials and using the software as often as possible will help you gain proficiency more quickly. If you have run through all the training the software company and your firm have, put your situation through the planning software to give yourself a better feel for the inputs and outputs.

Once you're comfortable, you'll be able to offer suggestions for improving day-to-day efficiency. Keep an eye out for software that may complement or replace what your firm is using.

What are other firms relying on? Your network can tell you.

Ask if you can attend a conference focused on technology for financial planners. Technology Tools for Today (T3) and Envestnet Advisor Summit are great options.

2 — Look for These Opportunities

The most successful new financial planners are continually looking for ways to improve themselves and add value to their organizations.

There's plenty of work to do before and after client meetings. This can include market research, analyzing client information, and coordinating post-meeting follow-ups. Look for client accounts that need rebalancing or are due for an update meeting. Review existing client documents to identify areas for improvement.

If you're working in a support role, ask to assist with the business development events. You'll quickly learn how difficult that part of the business can be and will be extra appreciative and respectful of those who can do it well. Observe more experienced advisors working with clients. Use what you've learned to develop your style with clients.

Look for marketing opportunities like managing the firm's website and social media and attending conferences like The Lean Startup to network with younger entrepreneurs whom no one wants to work with right now because they don't have millions in investable assets, but could make it big someday. Always try to be in the "what can I keep off my supervisor's plate" mindset. I remember one time when I started getting disgruntled with my boss early on in my career because I naively thought my job, putting together all the financial plans, was harder than his job of bringing in the clients. He taught me a lesson that I will never forget. I approached him about it, and he said, "okay, let's switch roles for one day. I will work on the two financial plans you have in progress, and you will go to the Chamber of Commerce event, Rotary event, and Business Networking group meetings tomorrow to pitch our firm and services." I was so excited, yay! I now get to be out of the office and not crunching plans. Little did I know that there were dozens of other financial planners at these meetings, much older and more experienced than me, and when it was my turn to stand up to speak, I failed miserably. Ouch.

3 — Day-To-Day Life at a Firm

What can you expect day-to-day? Financial planning is a service-oriented business. A lot of your time will consist of internal meetings, client meetings, team training, and the implementation of the advice you provide to clients. Remember the client pays the bills, and the sooner you develop a client-centered mentality, the better.

Always maintain a sense of urgency and approach each task as if it is not completed right then, your firm might lose the client.

4 — Maintain a Work-Life Blend

Initially, the workload may be heavy. Typically, you'll be busy from January through April and again from September through the middle of November. Summer will give you time to catch up and recharge.

You could work as much as 50–60 hours per week during busy periods and closer to 35–40 hours per week during off-peak times. Don't expect to go home every day at 5 p.m. Sometimes delivering what's been promised requires staying late to finish your work.

What's the key to a good work-life balance? Don't bring work home with you. Establish priorities for each day at the beginning of the week. And set longer-term priorities for the following weeks to stay on track. Maintain boundaries. If you need help creating a better work-life balance, talk to your manager.

Don't be afraid to speak up if you're feeling overworked. If you need help, ask for it. If your workload is too large, ask for a deadline extension. Missing deadlines and not communicating with your manager in advance will only cause bigger problems.

Self-care is critical. Take time to think and reflect. Work out the mind, body, and spirit. Don't skip meals to spend extra time working. Avoid social media during work hours because it will distract you and inhibit productivity.

5 — Professional Development

Professional development is critical to long-term success. Here are six hacks for staying professionally sharp.

#1 — Pursue the CFP® certification and other necessary licensure.

The CFP® certification demonstrates a commitment to the profession and a minimum level of technical competency. Then, as your career progresses, you can narrow your focus and pursue additional credentials later. To give financial advice and receive compensation for the advice, you will need the SIE, Series 7, and/or Series 65. Most firms will give you 3–12 months to pass these tests. More details on this are in Chapter 11.

#2 — Build real-world experience. Attend the Financial Planning Association's Residency Program. Plus the aforementioned Planning Zoo, Amplified Planning, and Financial Planning Externship.

#3 — Attend training. If your firm offers employee training, take advantage of the opportunity to refine your skills and acquire new ones. If they don't offer them, develop a list of events you would like to attend and propose them in a professional way to your manager. To ensure your manager sees the benefit of you gaining additional training and building your skills.

#4 — Gain leadership experience. Earn a seat on the board of your local Financial Planning Association chapter. And if that's not possible, join a committee. This will offer leadership experience, networking, and learning opportunities. Consider joining your local Homeowner Owners Association or Housing Authority for your Condo or Apartment so you can garner additional experience setting the vision,

leading, delegating, and managing people. If you are into physical fitness, you can join F3, which is a workout group for men that stands for Fitness, Fellowship, and Faith. It is a peer-led workout, so you will be forced to gain leadership skills if you become a part of a group. There is also a similar group for women called FIA Nation.

#5 — Volunteer. Serving your neighborhood association will further sharpen your management skills. Volunteering at a crisis call center will offer practice in helping people through stressful situations. This experience will be invaluable during market fluctuations or when dealing with clients' financial issues.

#6 — Become a stronger public speaker. Join your local Toastmasters chapter to sharpen your public speaking skills. You can also practice speaking at the local Chamber of Commerce and Rotary events. You need to strive to be able to speak impromptu at any given time and be able to control a crowd and take command of your audience.

***

The first 90 days of any job will involve a certain level of uncertainty. But it doesn't have to be overwhelming. By setting yourself up for success, avoiding common mistakes, looking for opportunities, maintaining a work-life balance, and focusing on professional development, you'll stay ahead.

Key Takeaways

- You have a lot to learn in a short amount of time.

- Every day that goes by, you are gaining momentum to get to where you want to go.

- Starting out can seem overwhelming, but stay patient.

- Be careful trying to take on too much at once.

Action Items

- Review Chapter 10 Materials using this QR Code.

- Pose the following question to yourself: how can I add value to this organization based on my skillset right now?

CHAPTER 11

— · —

INSIDER TIPS TO MAKING YOURSELF INDISPENSABLE TO FIRMS

"The only way to get what you're worth is to stand out, to exert emotional labor, to be seen as indispensable, and to produce interactions that organizations and people care deeply about."
—Seth Godin

Passing your appropriate licensing exams as quickly as possible will catapult your career to new heights. The sooner you get licensed, the sooner you can start adding value. As we discussed in Chapter 2, your licensing requirements will depend on what channel and firm structure you choose.

Securing the Series 65

The Series 65 will qualify you as an Investment Advisor Representative. You do not need a sponsor to take Series 65, so you could even take it before joining the organization. Currently, the exam consists of 130 questions and you're given 180 minutes to complete the exam, and the fee is $175.[1]

---

1. https://www.finra.org/registration-exams-ce/qualification-exams/series65

Currently, the exam is broken up into four sections as follows:[2]

- Economic Factors and Business Information — 15% or 20 questions

- Investment Vehicle Characteristics — 25% or 32 questions

- Client Investment Recommendations and Strategies — 30% or 39 questions

- Laws, Regulations, and Guidelines — 30% or 39 questions

Securing this license legally enables you to begin speaking with clients and providing investment advice immediately. If you delay in pursuing this license, your client interaction could be limited. This also demonstrates your initiative toward your new coworkers and supervisor.

Finally, there are undergraduate students in the various CFP® programs who are graduating with their Series 65. Once word spreads among the hiring firms, this will eventually become a minimum standard for a new planner entry-level financial hire candidate looking to go the Fee-only RIA route. You can do it!

Here is a story of how Corban Galloway, a recent graduate, passed the Series 65 on his first attempt:

"After reading some recommendations for study courses from the Series66 subreddit, I signed up for the Achievable Series 65 course and the Brian Lee's Series 65 course at TestGeek. Achievable provided a textbook with a good user interface that covered all the subjects on the exam and practice exams with a 2,200 possible question bank. It also

---

2. You can find review providers here: https://www.nasaa.org/exams/study-material-vendors/

has a timetable feature that helps you plan for how many study tasks to complete in a day to take the Series 65 by a certain date. The video course at TestGeek with Brian Lee was exceedingly practical in nature. Brian goes through key concepts and presents them in an easy-to-understand way. He also presents estimates for how many questions the Series 65 may have on a particular topic, points out questions that are almost always on the exam, and goes over some "tricks" that the question writers of the exam may use to confuse the test taker. The course has two practice exams of 130 questions each. In my situation, I felt the material on the Series 65 was a refresher from my Financial Planning classes and from my CFP Exam prep course, so I ended up not using Achievable hardly at all, as that course is better suited to establishing foundational learning of financial concepts. The TestGeek course, however, taught me what to expect on the exam and how to take it. My main study method is one that studies have shown to be the most effective: Write it down by hand. You can't write everything down, so focus on writing down the questions and answers for every question you get wrong or are unsure of on your practice exam. If you don't understand why the correct answer is correct, view the answer key explanation and delve into the topic further. I kept repeating this until I had the concepts ingrained into memory. I believe I studied for around a month or month and a half."

Securing the Securities Industry Essentials (SIE)

If you are looking at the wirehouse, insurance, broker-dealer, fee-based RIA channels, the SIE is more of an entry-level license to work your way up to a qualification examination such as the Series 7 which will be required to deliver investment advice and to receive a commission with a FINRA regulated firm.

For the SIE, there are 75 questions, the maximum time limit is 105 minutes, and the cost is $60. You do not need to be associated with any FINRA-registered firm to take the SIE.

Currently, the SIE is broken up into four categories:[3]

- Knowledge of Capital Markets - 16% or 12 questions

- Understanding Products and Their Risks - 44% or 33 questions

- Understanding Trading, Customer Accounts and Prohibited Activities - 31% or 23 questions

- Overview of Regulatory Framework - 9% or seven questions

After you pass the exam, you will need to be associated with a FINRA registered firm so they can "sponsor" you to take the Series 7.

Here are three stories of college students who passed the SIE on their first try while still in school:

"With more firms wanting the SIE when you start working for them, I decided to take it before I started applying for jobs. When studying for the SIE, since most of our classes cover the material in the SIE, I decided to just use free online practice exams for a couple of weeks before. The FINRA website has one free exam that is like the exam and a great tool. I also used other free online practice exams that helped me feel more prepared. I think this is a good cost-efficient way for college students to prepare for the SIE. Currently, I am studying for Series 65. For this exam, I am studying about two hours a day. I am using the Kaplan study material like the book and practice quizzes."—Shane Kozusko

"When I was studying for the SIE, the most helpful resources for me were the online practice exams. I started by reviewing FINRA's content

---

3. https://www.finra.org/registration-exams-ce/qualification-exam s/securities-industry-essentials-exam

outline for the exam, which allowed me to gauge how much I needed to study and what I needed to focus on. After that, I took several timed practice tests, which helped me get a feel for the format and pacing of the exam. After each exam, I would review the questions I got wrong and research the correct answer; doing so allowed me to study material I knew would likely be on the actual exam and learn more about things I was not taught in class. By repeating this process with different exams, I was able to review what I already knew and research relevant topics that I did not know. FINRA's website has a free SIE practice exam, but a quick Google search will yield lots more."—Josh Brumbach

"To prepare for the SIE, I set aside time for one week to study and take practice tests. I relied on the Financial Planning coursework I had already completed and chose to spend most of my time learning about the regulatory environment and laws that surround the securities industry. In the last three days before the exam date, I used practice exams to prepare for the test-taking experience and find gaps in my knowledge. I did not use any specific curriculum to study. I used my school textbooks, the SIE website guide, and free practice exams I found online. Using this method, I passed the exam on my first attempt."—Landon Powell

Series 7 Overview

Here is an overview of the four main current job functions the Series 7 covers:[4]

- F1 — Seeks Business for The Broker-Dealer from Customers and Potential Customers —7% or nine questions

- F2 — Opens Accounts After Obtaining and Evaluating Customers' Financial Profile and Investment Objectives —

---

4. https://www.finra.org/registration-exams-ce/qualification-exams/series7

9% or 11 questions

- F3 — Provides Customers with Information About Investments, Makes Recommendations, Transfers Assets and Maintains Appropriate Records—73% or 91 questions

- F4 — Obtains and Verifies Customers' Purchases and Sales Instructions and Agreements; Processes, Completes and Confirms Transactions—11% or 14 questions

Remember the sooner you knock these out, the sooner you can start working directly with clients and advising them (if that is your goal)!

My When Times Get Tough Top Eleven List

In life, for anyone, times get tough. For financial planners, it's no different. You will experience some rough spots in your first 90 days. When that happens, remember Caleb's When Times Get Tough Top Eleven List. Will these tips help you be more indispensable? Perhaps. It really depends on you. So, when you're down and out, Repeat after me:

1. I will strive to increase my maturity and professionalism so that I perform beyond my years.

2. I will go well above and beyond the minimum requirements for the position and the tasks that someone delegates to me.

3. I will be aware that I am still relatively unproven and that the person who hires and/or mentors me is taking a risk. I will remember that I am far from knowing all I need to know to be a successful financial planner, even though I have a degree in financial planning.

4. I will work to show firm owners I am serious about the financial planning profession and becoming a better financial planner. I understand that when they know this about me, it reduces their risk in hiring and mentoring me so they can see a return on their investment in me.

5. I will do whatever it takes to pass all licensing exams so I can add massive value to my new organization.

6. I will remember that my firm owner shouldn't have to repeat themselves about fixing a mistake that I have made. And I will do my utmost not to repeat mistakes but to learn from them.

7. I will be humble and respectful in any ideas I provide to my firm owner, especially if they are unsolicited.

8. I will understand that my firm owner's career path differs from mine. I realize that I might not survive in the business if it weren't for their success and the opportunity they are providing.

9. I will never be satisfied with the status quo. I will always push myself to better the organization I am a part of and the client's assets that I am responsible for.

10. I will go to my firm owner regularly to ask how I am progressing and if I am meeting expectations or hopefully exceeding them. Are there other more complicated things I can work on to assist the organization, and if not, what areas do I need to improve in to increase their comfort level in delegating me higher level work?

11. I will be sensitive to the fact that this is not my business and that the firm owner has the final say, even if it is a decision with which I disagree.

Your first year in the profession is going to be awesome! You are going to have to work hard because there is a lot to learn, and the expectations are high. Still, with some proper planning, determination, and lots of curiosity, you can deliver results beyond your wildest expectations.

Here is a chart and some guidelines to help ensure your first year is on track.

Estimated New Planner Skill Development Timeline Year 1		
Learning the business	Growing Your Skills	Fully Contributing to the Organization
0−6 months	6−12 months	~12+ months

Professionalism

Learn how to ask questions the right way.

You will need to ask a lot of questions, but you don't want to be a burden on your coworkers and boss. Try to solve the problem yourself and then go to your point of contact with all your questions at once. Don't pepper your colleagues with questions throughout the day.

Maybe even ask to set a standing time each day to review. You need to be able to do this with clients too. Ensure you have all your questions ready when you have the client's attention. Once you have your chance, you can follow up with one more thing, but beyond that it makes you look unorganized which does not instill confidence.

Receive constructive criticism without becoming defensive.

By this point, you should have had at least one—but ideally four—reviews, one each quarter. Stay in the mindset of *"They are sharing this with me to help me get to where I want to go,"* or your mind can easily begin to wander into imposter syndrome, which is doubting yourself and beginning to think you don't have what it takes and fear that someone is going to uncover that you are a fake and don't belong. Everyone faces imposter syndrome at some point in their career. When you do, take a deep breath, close your eyes, remind yourself how hard you have worked and how far you have come, and that your future is going to be big. Check out *The Gap and The Gain*, written by Dr. Benjamin Hardy and Dan Sullivan. You can also perform a simple search for "Dealing With Imposter Syndrome" to see how many other people it impacts and how they have overcome it. Don't let this hinder you!

Learn what your co-workers do in the firm.

Your co-workers will take you more seriously if you commit to learning about them and how doing what they do, allows you to do what you do.

Learn how to say no.

This may sound crazy because conventional wisdom is to say yes to everything. Saying yes to everything does not make you a superhero. Instead, it makes you feel overwhelmed. And when that happens, burnout is close behind. You do need to prepare for a heavy workload.

Also, Groupthink is not a characteristic of successful companies, so don't try to conform by being a "yes" person. This is the safe option, but realize if you approach it with respect and professionalism, it is okay to disagree. Think about it; the firm may have hired you, in part, to bring a new perspective.

Technical Knowledge

You should have acquired or are working to acquire the following technical knowledge:

- Pass the Securities Industry Essentials (SIE)

- Pass the Series 7 and/or Series 65 depending on how your firm is structured

- Sit for and Pass the CFP® certification examination

- Strong command of the basic concepts and technical areas of financial planning that you can effectively explain to clients/prospects

- Time value of money

- Cost of funds: pay off mortgage vs. invest

- Buy vs. rent

- Lease vs. finance

- Taxable vs. Tax deferred

- Asset location (placement of growth assets vs. assets that generate interest and dividends)

- Asset class allocation

- Cash flow management

- Purchasing home

- Refinancing home

- Insurance coverage needs analyses

- Know when you don't have all the information to answer the client's question

- Have the awareness to get your senior planner involved if it is a more complicated question

- Have a general understanding of all of the software and systems the firm employs

Communication

This is what financial planning is all about. You must be able to get clients to do what you want them to, even when they don't want to, then make them think it was their idea to do what you said they should do!

People are much more likely to act when they think it is their idea and not someone else's. If you can master this, you can be a successful financial planner. In the early stages of your career, you will find yourself knowing *what* to say. The thing you need to work on is *how* and *when* to say it. This takes lots of practice. Here are some guidelines for you to strive for:

- Have a general understanding of the backstory of each of the clients you are assigned to help serve and/or, depending on the size of the firm, the top 25% of client situations.

- Be able to tell a new acquaintance what you do and the services your firm provides in 30 seconds or less.

- Participate, at least as a note taker, in all types of client meetings (initial, discovery, brainstorming, plan presentation, e tc.).

- Draft a professional letter or email without a senior planner having to edit for spelling and grammar.

- Call clients directly to get the information you need and ensure it is a delightful experience for them.

- Manage your calendar and be able to schedule clients and prospects with appropriate lead time and pre and post-meeting time buffers.

- Conduct at least a portion of the Discovery/Data Gathering meeting call with clients and request basic information.

Present at least one item on the plan presentation meeting agenda. The cash flow or college funding areas are good places to start, and whatever else you enjoy and feel very confident in delivering to a client.

Here are some other resources and tools for you to consider in improving your client communication skills:

Money Quotient — https://www.moneyquotient.com/ — This company was started by Carol Anderson and is now run by her and her daughter, Amy Mullen, CFP®. They offer advanced training in client communication so financial planners can develop deeper, more fulfilling relationships with their clients and create more engaged clients who act upon the advice. They are based in Portland, OR, and to access their research, resources, and tools, you must be Money Quotient trained, which involves a three-day workshop with detailed instruction and practice in MQ True Wealth Process. I have been through this training, and it has helped me listen to clients more effectively, create deeper relationships with them, and give them better advice.

Sudden Money Institute — https://suddenmoney.com/ — Was originally founded by Susan Bradley, now a retired CERTIFIED FINANCIAL PLANNER™. Who had a niche clientele of people who received unexpected financial windfalls. When dealing with these clients, Susan realized their challenges needed to be addressed differently and has been training financial planners on exactly how to do that for the last few decades. You can earn a CeFT Certified Financial Transitionist credential from the Institute, which is a highly specialized but highly respected credential in the field.

Kinder Institute — https://www.kinderinstitute.com/ — Founded by George Kinder, CFP® and Susan Galvan and now run solely by George Kinder is a training company dedicated to helping financial planners implement financial life planning with their clients. Their signature intensive training—the EVOKE process and the Registered Life Planner (RLP) certification can be instrumental in understanding clients at a deeper level so financial planners can tailor the advice so the clients act upon it.

Mitch Anthony — https://www.mitchanthony.com/ — Founded by Mitch Anthony, a coach, consultant, speaker, and trainer whose books and resources help financial planners engage more deeply with their current clients but also secure new clients.

***

The first year of your professional life is a big deal, and it is okay to feel different emotions, from fear and anxiety to exuberance! Follow these tips, and don't get too caught up in getting everything right.

Also, as you progress throughout the year, be sure to reflect on how far you have come. Use that as your measuring stick to gauge how far you have come versus how far you have to go which can easily become discouraging.

Key Takeaways

- You have to be licensed to give investment advice and provide financial planning.

- Focus on learning the technical component of the job when first starting.

- Deal with any imposter syndrome feelings head on.

- Use the confidence you are building in the technical areas of financial planning to begin increasing your confidence with the communication component.

Action Items

- Review Chapter 11 Materials using this QR Code.

- Listen to The New Planner Podcast episode #89 with Shane Kozusko on how to pass the Series 65. https://newplannerrecruiting.com/ep-89-how-to-pass-the-series-65-exam-with-shane-kozusko/

- Review all the free resources available from Money Quotient, Sudden Money Institute, Kinder Institute, and Mitch Anthony.

CHAPTER 12

— · —

YOUR GUIDE TO PASSING THE CFP® EXAM THE FIRST TIME

"Our potential is one thing. What we do with it is quite another."
—Angela Duckworth

As financial planning continues its march towards becoming a globally recognized profession, the CERTIFIED FINANCIAL PLANNER™ designation has become the baseline standard for aspiring financial planners.

To attain the CFP® "marks," you must complete specific courses within a CFP Board registered program, pass a comprehensive exam, meet one of two minimum experience requirements, and meet ethics requirements. The first CFP® exam, a two-day "paper" exam consisting of multiple-choice questions and written responses, was offered in 1991 and has evolved with the financial planning profession. The exam is now a computer-based 170 question multiple-choice exam delivered over two three-hour sessions that are completed in one day.

Each question has four answer choices, and there are no essays or written response questions. There is, however, at least one case study that precedes a series of multiple-choice questions. The content includes professional conduct and regulation, general principles of financial planning, estate, tax, investment, retirement, risk management, and insurance planning.

The exam confirms technical competency and tests one's ability to apply that knowledge in practical scenarios. Exam questions are written by volunteer subject matter experts in the field of financial planning. The overall pass rate typically hovers between 60%–65%, with first-time test takers fairing slightly better. The exam is typically offered at Prometric testing centers in March, July, and November. With the COVID-19 pandemic promoting innovation across the globe, the CFP Board announced that the exam would be temporarily offered remotely.

It's important to note that the CFP® designation isn't legally required to "hang a shingle" and practice financial planning. It is a voluntary certification. As previously mentioned, those legal requirements are dependent on the services and products provided, the size of the firm, and the state in which the business operates. You can still call yourself a financial planner even if you do not have the CFP® certification; you wouldn't be able to refer to yourself as a CFP® professional though.

Though the CFP® designation is a substitute, to become an Investment Advisor Representative (IAR) of an RIA for the Series 65 in many states, attaining the CFP® "mark" demonstrates core financial planning competency and carries the responsibility of fiduciary advice. Further, it elevates a professional's standing with the American public and within the profession. It is currently considered the gold standard for financial planner certifications

The Decision

Deciding when to take the exam is among the most important considerations of this process.

It's a question I get often: *"Should I take the exam as soon as I complete the CFP® coursework, or gain experience first?"*

Like most answers to questions of this magnitude, it depends on the individual. Countless candidates have completed the exam with both approaches. In general, for strong students graduating from a top-tier financial planning program, their best bet is to complete a review course and sit for the exam within one year of graduation.

The technical skills are still fresh, the tax laws memorized in school remain current, and the process of studying is still a natural part of the routine. For recent graduates who struggled with the coursework, those overwhelmed by responsibilities inside or outside of the office, or professionals who are still identifying the "why" in financial planning concepts, waiting to sit for the exam may be their best option. All of this, of course, is dependent on the individual and is a decision that should be made with the help of sincere counsel.

Job seekers often ask, *"Should I take the CFP® exam once just to see what's on it?"* But this isn't the best approach. Not only does the CFP® exam cost $925, but a solid review course will also provide better, easier-to-retain information about what is on the exam. Passing the CFP® exam requires a great deal of commitment. You should decide to *pass* the exam rather than merely sit for it. While the exam's core is consistent, each testing cycle is unique. There is no guarantee that taking the exam in March will truly prepare you for the exam in July. It is also better if you can tell potential employers that you passed the exam on the first attempt.

Hurdles to Taking Directly After Graduation

First, cost. It's currently $925 for a standard registration per attempt or $825 if you register more than six weeks ahead of the exam date. The cost goes up to $1,025 if you register within six weeks. Signing up early helps save you money but also improves your psyche since you are much more likely to accomplish a goal that you write down, see every day, and associate a deadline to. The exam could be free to you if you apply and are awarded one of the CFP Board Scholarships.[1] Next, if you haven't had the opportunity to see many financial planning situations and provide advice on those situations, it is going to be difficult to pass since that is the makeup of most questions.

Benefits to Taking Directly After Graduation

First, the information is fresh in your mind. Second, you likely have not started your full-time job yet, thus giving you time and flexibility in your study plan. Finally, you can be more marketable to a potential employer if you can say you have taken and passed the exam. This solidifies your skill set, passion, and commitment to the profession.

Hurdles to waiting until after becoming employed

You may become so immersed in learning a new position, new firm, and adjusting to being out of college you cannot focus on preparing for the exam.

Just because you might be employed full-time in a financial planning firm does not necessarily mean you will be working with clients on analyzing situations and developing strategies.

Benefits to waiting until after becoming employed

First, you would have access to other senior advisors who can coach and mentor you on what to expect, provide real-life case studies, or simply help with everyday client planning work to gain confidence and experience. Next, you might have the opportunity to work on client situations, better preparing you for the questions you will face. Finally, waiting might allow you to have the exam and exam prep materials paid for as part of your compensation. Although the statistics show

---

1. https://www.cfp.net/get-certified/tools-and-resources/apply-f or-a-scholarship

that when you do not pay for the exam and materials yourself, you tend not to fare as well as your counterparts who did.

Preparation

Determining how to prepare for the exam is important. Like most things in life, creating a disciplined structured plan and sticking to it is vital. Everyone learns differently, and each person must determine what type of learner they are.

There are three types of learners: Visual, Auditory, and Kinesthetic.

Visual learners, of course, learn best by observing others. Auditory learners best learn by listening to instruction. Those who learn best by doing are typically described as kinesthetic learners.

I encourage candidates to find an online quiz or take the time to consider how they most effectively learn the material. This will go a long way in creating a cohesive study plan.

In our recruiting firm, we speak with hundreds of candidates every year who are successful in passing the CFP® exam and many others who are not. We have found that candidates who are successful in passing the exam share the following characteristics:

- They commit to a structured study routine and maintain consistent discipline throughout the process.

- They prioritize their exam for at least three months and have "buy-in" from their personal and professional support systems.

- They focus on what they don't know rather than what they do. It's tempting to overstudy for the topics you enjoy or are most comfortable with. We all love financial planning and never miss an opportunity to "nerd out" on our favorite topic. But remember, your goal is to pass the exam. It's important to go into the exam with a balanced understanding of the material. You will have the rest of your career to develop more nuanced expertise!

"The exam is very difficult. I am glad I found a firm to work for that sees the value in the CFP® certification and encouraged me to pursue it. And has given me flexibility to study and meet with my mentors to go over strategies and concepts I needed to strengthen."

—Alison S., Passed exam on first attempt

On the other hand, students who do not pass the exam typically demonstrate the following characteristics:

- They underestimate the difficulty and rigor of the exam.

- They do not take it seriously or feel forced to take it.

- They rely too much on professional experience and not enough on the review material.

- They spend too much time studying material they already understand.

- They have too many personal and professional distractions to spend an adequate amount of time preparing for the exam.

It's important to note that there is no single approach that guarantees you'll pass the exam the first try, but the aforementioned items are good indicators. There are certainly underprepared individuals who pass and well-prepared individuals who do not. Many intelligent, diligent, test takers fail the exam each testing cycle. Passage or failure of the CFP® exam is not a permanent indication of your ability to thrive in the profession.

A review course can be one of the most important ingredients of your study plan. We're asked daily whether a review course is worth the investment, and our answer is almost always, "Yes." Technical expertise in financial planning and mastery of the approach to the CFP® exam is not necessarily the same thing. The purpose of these courses isn't to teach you the material but to provide you with the tools, structure, and forced discipline to pass the exam.

The CFP Board currently lists over a dozen review courses each offering a unique approach to preparing for the exam.[2] Most review courses offer some combination of the review material, practice questions, and feedback specific to your strengths and weaknesses.

Some offer asynchronous review sessions or lectures, others offer periodic live review sessions, and others a condensed "live review." Spend some time researching each program and ask successful test-takers in your network what they recommend. Make sure you create an account with the CFP Board and visit the Candidate Forum, where you will find lots of very detailed study plans and review provider advice. Be sure that the delivery format matches your learning style, and be sure to inquire about the program's pass rate.

Some review courses also offer "guarantees" or additional coaching should your first attempt prove unsuccessful. Regardless of which review course you choose, it's important to exhaust the provided materials and trust the study plan.

Once a test date and review course have been chosen, it's time to get started. You must determine how much and how long you intend to prepare for the exam. After speaking with thousands of successful test-takers across the nation, we encourage at least three to five months

---

2.

https://www.cfp.net/get-certified/certification-process/exam-requirement/cfp-exam-preparation/exam-prep-resources/cfp-exam-review-courses of focused study. This will include daily study, as much as 2 hours per weekday, with more intense study occurring during weekends. Some test-takers will need to study more than that, of course, and honest self-assessment is requisite to effective preparation. Should you choose to purchase a review course, you will be provided with a study plan specific to their materials.

The CFP Board offers a free practice test to everyone who registers for the exam. It may be best to start with this exam to set a baseline for areas in which you need to improve. Perhaps you struggle with estate planning; taking a pretest will uncover specific deficiencies in your knowledge. Be sure to spend additional time reviewing these concepts and working through difficult practice problems. Remember, it's better to study for a couple of hours every day rather than cram at the last minute.

It's also important to be mindful of how much each topic is tested on the exam. This is vital to assign the appropriate amount of time to each core area of the exam. According to the CFP Board, the exam is broken down as follows:[3]

- Professional conduct and regulation — 8%

- General principles of financial planning — 15%

- Psychology of Financial Planning — 7%

- Risk management and insurance planning — 11%

- Investment planning — 17%

- Tax planning — 14%

---

3. https://www.cfp.net/get-certified/certification-process/exam-requirement

- Retirement savings and income planning — 18%

- Estate planning — 10%

Many candidates overlook the general principles and professional conduct sections of the material. These sections cover the basic regulatory framework, the financial planning process, and the maintenance of the CFP® mark. You must get these questions right. Further, don't skim over the areas you feel are not as important as the heavier technical areas. Nothing invokes panic during an exam as much as floundering on a question you "should" know the answer to.

As you work through the study material, make sure you focus on learning, not just memorizing the material. The exam tests your ability to apply knowledge more so than the knowledge itself. Make sure you understand the *why* in the correct answer. Also, work through as many practice questions as you can. You'll feel most confident if you can apply your knowledge to tackle questions in any way the CFP Board throws them at you. For many questions, the correct answer is the exception to the rule. So, it is important to apply what you have learned.

As you get closer to exam time, you should have a solid grasp of the material, have taken multiple practice exams, and should be refining your knowledge in those remaining trouble areas. During the final two weeks, the heavy studying you did early on should be paying off, and developing confidence should be your focus.

At this juncture, it's too late to cram. Take time to review the basics one last time and spend one final day on each topic area. Get plenty of sleep, and don't make the mistake of taking a practice exam the day before the real thing. Not only will you be mentally exhausted, but you also don't want your confidence rattled this close to exam time.

If you have the option to take the day off before the exam, it may be a good idea to do so. Spend a couple of hours that morning reviewing concepts and do something relaxing that afternoon. Eating a healthy meal for dinner, going to bed early, and turning off screens will ensure you're mentally prepared for the big day!

On the morning of the exam, be sure to allow plenty of time to get to the testing center, eat a healthy breakfast, and remember to pack a lunch. You will not be able to bring food or beverages into the exam, so pack items you can leave in a vehicle or locker.

Remember, you're entitled to a 40-minute break between the three-hour exam sessions. If you have a favorite candy bar or treat, put one in your lunch as a reward for completing the first half of the exam. You must remember your calculator and a valid, government-issued ID. It's prudent to have a "backup" calculator on hand as well.

The CFP Board clearly states that you are allowed "one or more battery-powered, non-programmable, dedicated financial function c alculators."[4] If you have two calculators, bring them both, and if you only have one, be sure it has fresh batteries. We've heard many stories of candidates showing up to the testing site and forgetting a basic item, like an ID or calculator. Once you sit down to begin the exam, take a deep breath, and relax. At this point, it's all about focus and execution.

After completing your exam, you'll receive an email from Prometric providing one of two results.

Preliminary Pass! Congratulations, after months of study and sacrifice, you've taken a major step in your career. It's time to share this moment with family, friends, mentors, and colleagues. This is a huge milestone in your career. You will receive official results approximate-

4. https://www.cfp.net/get-certified/certification-process/exam-r equirement/about-the-cfp-exam/what-to-expect-on-exam-day

ly four weeks from your test date. You do not immediately become a CFP® certificant upon passage of the exam. You must meet the experience requirement, pay the applicable fee, and meet the ethics requirement to use the marks after your name.

If you did not meet the minimum score to receive a preliminary pass, you will receive a diagnostic report of your performance in each topic area. This does not mean you don't have what it takes to be a great planner, so don't give up! Save the diagnostic report and take a couple of days to process the results before charting a path forward. Try not to fret too much; no reasonable employer is going to hold it against you if you fail the exam once before passing.

Many review material providers offer one-on-one counseling to help you tackle your next attempt at the exam and may allow you to retake the review course at reduced or no charge. Once you receive the official results, you can decide whether the time is right to retake the exam.

The CFP Board's retake policy is straightforward. You must wait until the next testing window opens (i.e., you cannot take the March exam twice) and may only attempt the exam three times in a twenty-four-month window. The CFP Board only allows test-takers five total attempts at passing the exam.[5] Be mindful, but not fearful, of this policy.

Successfully attaining the CFP® "mark" is no small task. The coursework entails quantitative challenge and emotional nuance. Passing the exam requires shrewd discipline in both scheduling and focus.

The payoff, however, is well worth the sacrifice. Not only will you set yourself apart in the job market, but you'll also find yourself one

---

5. https://www.cfp.net/get-certified/tools-and-resources/faqs

step closer to fulfilling the ultimate aspiration: using your financial planning knowledge to impact clients and help them achieve their goals.

Do's and Don'ts When Preparing for the CFP® Exam

By now, you've come to expect me to offer you some advice to set you up for success. Well, I'm not going to disappoint you. Review the following tips for prepping for the CFP® exam and it will increase your odds of passing. I'm not guaranteeing you'll pass, but I can guarantee they will help in your preparation.

These are Must Do's

Set expectations — Make sure you understand the magnitude of the exam. It's rigorous. Pursuing an undertaking of this significance is not for everybody. It will require discipline and hard work for a favorable outcome. You must have time to prepare. Planning a wedding, remodeling a home, taking a trip around the world, etc., while studying is not suggested.

Develop a routine — Especially for those who lack organization and need structure. A set routine is an absolute must for an undertaking such as the CFP® exam and will keep you motivated when you do not feel like studying. Put placeholders in your calendar to block off designated study times and set alarms on your phone to help remind you and keep you on track.

Here's how I approached the exam.

I graduated in December and planned to take the July exam. I purchased the review materials in April and began working on questions on my own before the live review, which began in June. I studied about four hours per day, usually an hour in the morning, one hour during lunch, and a couple of hours in the evening.

I took one day off during the weekend.

When the review course started, we met three nights per week for two hours and were assigned readings and question sets on the off nights. The first two weekends in July were intensive study sessions set aside for case studies and practice tests.

Frankly, the greatest benefit I received from the live review was it forced me to study and stay on schedule. Just so you have a reference point, I spent about 350 hours in total preparing.

Create an organized study plan — There are lots of guides in the study materials provided by the various industry vendors. If you are not careful about planning your study time and setting incremental goals and are not structured, your study plan is doomed before it even begins.

What did I do?

I read the chapters first, then worked through the questions. I created an answer sheet that I have included in the resources section that I used so I could track any trends that developed. In the answer sheet, I had a space for comments where I wrote out the full correct answer to questions I missed.

To train my mind to move from one topic to another seamlessly, when I read a section about stock options, I would then turn to a non-associated question area such as estate or life insurance planning. The continual shifting between topics helped prepare me for the random order of topics on the exam.

Although many students purchased commercially prepared flashcards to quiz themselves, I created my flashcards. The process of making the flashcards helped solidify the information for me. This is one example of how the study plan should be tailored to individual learning styles and preferences—visual learner, conceptual, or kinesthetic. Know thyself, friend. And prepare accordingly.

Focus on weaker areas first — You should attack the areas you are the weakest in and plan to spend the most time shoring up these areas. This is difficult as most test takers will want to focus on the topics they know the best. I did not particularly care for estate and tax planning and knew I had a long way to go in those areas before the big day. So, I built that into my study plan. I made those areas my top priorities and worked my way down the list of technical subjects. I ended up reviewing the topics I enjoyed the most and was strongest in last.

Use multiple review providers' materials — The more questions you can work on, the higher the chance of success.

Did I follow my advice?

Once I had completed all the questions in the primary review materials twice, I purchased additional review materials from another vendor. This is important because the tendency is to get used to the way questions are being asked. When you do, you lose the ability to accurately study the material due to developing certain biases. You avoid getting too familiar with the way one company asks questions.[6]

Utilize your network of alumni or local FPA/NAPFA chapter for assistance — Find CFP® practitioners whom you can ask to mentor you to help prepare for the real-life questions you will face.

I visited Bryan's office, where I was going to work after the exam. He would quiz me on client situations and ask me what I would do and why type questions. This helped me prepare. I remember, during one of our sessions, we were talking about the holding periods for stock options to be taxed at long-term capital gains rates, and I incorrectly said something like you have to hold for a year. Bryan pointed out that I would have missed that question because it has to be held for

---

6. For some information on the review providers, visit http://new-plannerrecruiting.com/resources/

longer than a year as written in the tax code. You probably knew that already and wouldn't have been tripped up like I was. This helped me understand how much thought I had to put into each question and how many technical areas I might have to draw from.

The test is difficult for aspiring planners, especially those without experience, because most questions are structured as, "If a client walks in and has this, or says this, based on what you know about their situation, what would you recommend?" You must know the material thoroughly to get these types of questions right.

Read the questions very carefully — Watch the exception to the exception. The questions are fair even though most of them have several answers that could work, but the exam writers want to test your knowledge to select the *best* answer.

What was my experience?

Some of my exam study peers would read the answers to the question before reading the question, and some had success with that method. I just made sure I read the question multiple times, the first time at normal speed and the second time at less speed. During the multiple readings, I tried to develop my answers before looking at the answer choices and thought about ways the test writers could be trying to lead me astray.

Watch your time — There will be short scenarios (mini case studies) and comprehensive case studies in each test session. These can consume a lot of time if you aren't careful because there can be quite a bit of irrelevant information given. Managing time well is critical. You should strive for 1.5 minutes per question during the practice study sessions.

Sometimes, you might not have time to read the questions twice, as I mentioned previously. If you don't know the answer to something, narrow it down the best you can and guess.

Here Are Some Don'ts

Take the exam for granted — Trying to cram at the last minute greatly reduces your odds of passing the exam. Also, relying on the live reviews instead of studying a regular amount each day will not suffice. Frankly, the battles are won and lost each day when you have focused study time and are going through the material and exam questions voraciously.

Get hung up on one question — Don't waste time by getting hung up on one question. If you come across something you have never seen, guess and move on.

I remember coming across a question on an investment instrument I had never heard of. It was not discussed in any of the review materials I had, so I calmly reminded myself not to let it shake me, guessed, and moved on.

You will encounter questions that you do not know how to answer. When you do, you must remember that you can afford to get some questions wrong. You are not going up against your peers next to you, and you don't have to achieve an arbitrary passing percentage such as 70%. The exam is instead scored on a modified Angoff system which scores test takers on a pre-established level of competency.[7]

Neglect your calculator skills — Even though there may be fewer calculation questions (a buzz I have heard recently), you need to have a thorough understanding of your financial calculator. Good mastery of your calculator can help you squeeze out a few extra points.

Be tempted to talk to other people to see how you did — After the first session, you will only get frustrated and discouraged

---

7. https://www.cfp.net/get-certified/certification-process/exam-re quirement/about-the-cfp-exam

trying to compare answers with others. You don't want to second guess yourself. You need to be positive going into the next section.

Panic! — When you are seated at your workstation and beginning, you would be wise to channel the nervous energy to give each question the time and attention it deserves. Positive thoughts and a *can-do attitude* are helpful here as well.

***

Finally, I would avoid trying to spend a lot of time listening to other people who are certain they can tell you what will be on the exam. The feedback that I have gotten from other people is like talking to an economist or weatherman—right about half the time and wrong about half the time.

I do feel those test takers should try to anticipate what they might see based on what trends are developing in the industry. I sense that there are now probably more questions about Medicare, long-term care, annuities, social security, college planning, debt, credit, and Exchange Traded Funds than there were when I took the exam many years ago.

Again, if you seek a full understanding of the material, you should do well. Also, realize that now that the exam is much shorter, with 115 fewer questions, there is very little room for obscure type questions that used to pop up frequently because the CFP Board still must test the core competencies and they have fewer questions to do so.

Key Takeaways

- The CFP® exam is a very rigorous professional examination.

- Shortcut slick test-taking strategies aren't a substitute for putting in the time and learning the material.

- Preparing for the exam will consume your life for at least a few months.

- You will have more confidence and garner more respect as a new planner when you pass.

Action Items

- Review Chapter 12 Materials using this QR Code.

- Apply for as many CFP® exam and educational reimbursement scholarships as you can find. There are lots of them! https://www.cfp.net/the-center-for-financial-plann ing/get-involved/ways-to-give/scholarships

- Take one practice exam before you start studying, take one in the middle, then take one a few weeks out from the real test.

CHAPTER 13

—·—

WHAT THE FUTURE HOLDS FOR YOU

"*Some people dream of success while others wake up and work.*"
— Winston Churchill

To enjoy a long and successful career in financial planning, you must master several areas which are: the technical, relational, sales, and firm management aspects of the job. Think of it as a four-legged stool and all legs must be strong.

In the beginning, the profession was focused primarily on the sales component. But as the industry has grown and moved into a full-fledged profession, it now more closely resembles other well-established professions, such as accounting, law, and medicine, where the initial key focus is developing the technical expertise, not selling.

When you start as a new financial planner, you will now have the option not to have to hunt for new clients to be paid. However, even with the emergence of this new career model, you will encounter firms that were founded by the first generation of financial planners. That generation sometimes expects you to start the same way they did. If this is appealing to you, you can certainly have a successful career going forward, but the sales only path is not the path of the future.

"Even though I thought the technical component was going to be the toughest to learn, I quickly found out it was the relationship and sales aspects that were the most difficult to develop and I am still working on them!"

—Mary A., CFP® with 5 years of experience

The founding generation started their careers learning sales and marketing, then progressed to technical competence. Now, as the graphic by Michael Kitces illustrates, the progression for newer planners is the opposite of what it once was.[1]

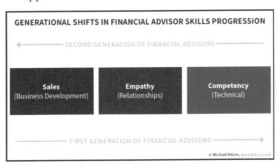

Assuming you can find a firm that will hire you under the apprenticeship financial planner model, you will need to build your skill set so you can move up the career ladder and proceed with your career.

It might take you a few years in the business to truly understand where your skills and passions lie. In most cases, you will know where you are the best fit after you have been in the Paraplanner and/or Associate Advisor position. As I have mentioned several times, one of the benefits of a career in financial planning is that you can start on one track and move to another. Once you have additional clarity on the direction you want to go, there are three main areas of focus within a firm that you could follow, which are:

---

1. See www.kitces.com for more information.

- <u>Relationship/Advisory Focus</u> — Spending the bulk of their time and career finding clients, building relationships with them and becoming the primary point of contact for the client.

- <u>Technical Focus</u> — Can be client-facing, but may not be depending on the size of the firm. Also may not have clients of their own; however, every technical question/topic stops at their desk. When the relationship track people have questions about a planning strategy or something their client brings up, the Director of Financial Planning is the go-to resource.

- <u>Management Focus</u> — I have seen many people over my career who thought they wanted to be on the relationship track, but after a few years, found out they didn't like having to talk to clients when the market was down. They loved the profession, though, and wanted to be involved, so they began to develop their management and leadership skills and went on to become COO, CEO, and CCO types.

"I started out on the operations side because I was nervous to talk to clients. Over the years though, I noticed how the planners in our office interacted with the clients and I wanted to have that so I started pursuing the CFP and moved into a paraplanner role."

—Mike J., Spent 5 years in operations before moving over to the advisory career track

The below chart describes each focus visually and also gives you some common position titles as you move up the track. This graph depicts someone starting in a paraplanner role on the relationship-focused track, then after a few years in the profession, having the option to move over to the Operations Manager or Analyst jobs.

Managerial	Relationship	Technical
Chief Executive Officer	Senior Planner	Director of Financial Planning
Chief Operations Officer		
Chief Compliance Officer	Lead Planner	Financial Planning Specialist
Director of Operations		
Operations Manager	Associate Planner	Analyst
	Paraplanner	

Realize too that you could start in a small firm and find yourself doing all these things as most firm owners in smaller firms do as well. To reiterate, the more exposure you get to these types of activities the earlier in your career, the faster you can figure out where to focus your efforts.

As your career progresses, depending on which area of focus you choose, you will be required to deepen your knowledge bench and work your way up. For example, on the relationship track, you will need to work up to handling the firm's largest and most complicated clients. Honing your skills so you can effectively guide even the most difficult of clients in terms of personality and communication style.

It is one thing to do all you are supposed to do to become a successful planner, but what separates the *good* planners from the *great* planners? Ed Jacobsen, the pioneer of Positive Financial Planning, teacher, author, and mentor who passed away in 2020, described what he saw as the differentiators in his article *The Core Skills of a Stellar Financial Planner,* which is included verbatim with permission here:

I recently facilitated a conversation about key skills and qualities of successful financial planners during a teleconference of FPA's Practitioner Advisory Council. I thought you might be interested in what

Council members (all of whom are experienced and mature planners, plus the occasional non-planner like myself) said. I know I'm interested in your thoughts about their thoughts.

To mine the wisdom of these experienced planners about the skills and qualities (apart from financial skills and technical acumen) they believe are key to their success, I posed two positive (aka: appreciative) questions:

> 1. As an experienced financial planner (and possibly a business owner), what are the most important skills you have developed and deepened that contribute to your success? (i.e., if that skill or quality were absent or poorly developed, you would not be nearly as successful)

> 2. Think about a great client relationship that you have: one that's successful by anyone's standards. What skills and qualities are you using in this relationship? What does the client appreciate and admire most about you and how you serve them? What do you do that matters most to the client and the relationship? And can you think of a "Tipping Point Moment" where the relationship deepened or got traction?

Here's a "composite profile" of the successful financial planner that emerged. See if it rings true. Does it sound like any planner you know? Does it sound like you? What would you add, modify, or delete to make it more accurate, complete, and useful?

Listens with Openness and Curiosity: seeks to understand (rather than to judge, analyze, or change) the client's values, goals, and perspectives; also, listens to understand the meanings beneath the client's words; is fully present with the client (aka refrains from silently rehearsing your response).

Empathy: senses what the client is feeling: is attuned to your bodily cues for clues about what client may be feeling—but stays emotionally balanced. (Note: recent neuroscience research shows that "mirror neurons" in the brain may be responsible for this kind of "felt empathy" for another person.)

"Gets" and Values the Client: this includes cognitive understanding, but also (i) a deeper "felt sense" of who this person is and (ii) caring about them (i.e., valuing their well-being). It's not unusual for clients to say to planners who deeply "get" them, "You know more about me than my spouse."

Participants translated the above qualities and skills into specific behavioral practices:

Cultivates a Safe Environment: creates a place where clients feel safe and trusting. It includes many of the above aspects: authentic, non-judgmental listening; truly seeking to understand, inviting the client to disclose and explore personally important information that may be relevant to their financial plans.

Uses Coaching Skills: refrains from "selling a solution" or directing the client. Instead, acts like a coach, guiding the client to make the decision that's in their best interest.

Is "On Alert" 24/7: several said they are always thinking (and sometimes even dream) about their clients. When they encounter information relevant to specific clients, many send it along with a brief "Thought this would interest you," which shows the client that their planner cares about them and is committed to their well-being.

Is Open, Self-aware, and Transparent: (i) says "I don't know" rather than faking it; (ii) apologizes for mistakes; (iii) delegates tasks (i.e., doesn't play Lone Ranger), either because planner doesn't excel at the task and/or because delegating increases productivity (and is a developmental opportunity). One planner posts a "Park Your Egos at the Door" sign on the conference room; and (iv) in addition to knowing their limits, has a secure understanding of the "sweet spots" in their skills, personal qualities, and experience base.

Acts Professionally, and Then Some: always keeps promises, follows up in a timely way, gets the details right. Moreover, one goes beyond the extra mile, showing up for the client in ways beyond anything in a "normal" profile. One example: driving a client to chemotherapy appointments.

There was broad Council consensus on the profile. There also was recognition that these so-called "soft skills" are not routinely taught in financial planning curricula—that planners are required to master (and keep up with) a complex world of financial theory, process, products, requirements, technology, and more. As one Council member put it, "*We have to have Big Brains and Soft Hearts.*"

***

Ed's wife and business partner Dr. Jody Jacobson continues to build upon Ed's legacy through the Human Skills Institute.[2]

I cannot stress enough how important developing your client relationship skills are towards your success as a financial planner. There are lots of things you need to know how to do, but at the end of the day, the financial planning profession is a people business. You must be able to master the skill of dealing with people to have long-term success. Dealing with people effectively can be a challenging skill for some to learn because human emotions are involved, and those don't fit nicely into a spreadsheet.

---

2. humanskillsinstitute.com

Growing Your Expertise for the Future

In terms of growing your technical expertise, here are some ideas for you to consider for what is next after the CFP® certification. There are two likely paths you could take.

The first path is that you begin pursuing subject matter expertise in certain areas to add value to your clients and your firm. When I started in the profession a long time ago, everyone said they were a subject matter expert in investments or retirement planning.

Since the investment management part of the business has become largely commoditized and outsourced via automatic rebalancer tools through Robo Advisors and Turnkey Asset Management Platforms (TAMPS), you should now look outside the traditional technical areas. Here are some ideas for you to consider and spur additional thought:

- **Entrepreneurship planning** — Helping your clients start businesses can be very valuable. Especially if they want to leave their corporate executive employee type role or if we encounter another pandemic as we did in 2020.

- **Career Development** — You can assist your clients in negotiating their salary and employee benefits package, find other offers at competing firms or act as a referral to a corporate recruiter, where they can leave a high-paying job for a not as high paying job that is more fulfilling to them.

- **Life Coaching** — When you start working with clients and assuming you are their trusted advisor, they will share many things with you. Be prepared to help guide them through the ups and downs of life, not just the stock market. Through mediation, conflict resolution, and transition training, you will be positioned to help them navigate death, divorce, retirement, job loss, anxiety, empty nest syndrome, and illness.

- **Common Coding Languages** — We are rapidly moving to a society where everyone needs to have some background knowledge of basic coding languages, even if you are not an IT type. You can add value in multiple ways with these skills, from updating websites and creating basic websites for your new entrepreneur client to troubleshooting internal software issues. It also gives you credibility with the software engineer or IT clients you have or will be targeting.

- **Digital Marketing** — It is common for firms to attract clients outside of their geographic region. Suppose you have an affinity for social media platforms, sales funnels, and email campaigns and can develop the strategy and implement that strategy across your firm. That is a skill set that is rare for most CERTIFIED FINANCIAL PLANNER™ practitioners

- **Virtual Team Management** — Managing people is hard, and most practitioners would rather not have to deal with it since they know their skill set is obtaining clients and solving the client's problems. Developing expertise in people management both in person and virtual (more challenging in virtual environments) can make you an invaluable team member very quickly.

The second path you might take is pursuing additional training, education, and credentialing centered around the clientele your firm already works with. Or, perhaps a clientele you want to target as part of your business development responsibilities.

Let me give you an example. If you join a firm that prepares taxes, securing the Enrolled Agent (EA) certification will increase your knowledge, confidence, and credibility with clients.

Here are some others:[3]

Niche Client or Core Service Area	Potential Certification
Retiree	RICP
Divorcees	CDFA
Insurance	CLU/CHFC
Ultra High Net Worth	CPWA
Investment Mgmt & Manager Selection	CFA, CIMA, or AIF
Employee Benefits	CEBS
Trusts	CTFA
College Planning	CCPS

Even though you may start your career without having to bring in clients, as your career progresses and your compensation increases, there will be some business development component. I think you will also find, as your career progresses, the act of bringing in clients, which may have frightened you and even made you apprehensive about the profession at first, will be much easier.

Bringing in clients is mostly about building trust and having confidence which will happen naturally throughout your career. Also, suppose you are an active member of your local and/or online community. In that case, it is inevitable that people will ask you what you do, which is a great segue into establishing a potential working relationship with them.

As the profession has progressed thus far, the financial planners who have zeroed in on a certain type of client where they already have

---

3. For a full list see, "Professional Designations | FINRA.Org," accessed February 18, 2022, https://www.finra.org/investors/p rofessional-designations.

an existing area of expertise or want to develop an area of expertise are having success. When seeking to develop a niche clientele, avoid the ones everyone else targets, namely *affluent clients, executives, small business owners, women*, and *pre-retirees.* Those are in a red ocean (lots of competition), and you want to operate in a blue ocean (not as much competition).[4]

Here are some ideas for niches that are not—at least yet—heavily pursued by the financial planning community:

- **Tech startups** — Most established firms are only interested in the founders or employees of startups after they have sold their business (liquidity event) or have massive amounts of stock options awarded to them. What about all the budding entrepreneurs out there who are working on the next Google, Facebook, or Microsoft? They need advice but don't necessarily have the assets to manage yet.

- **Physician Assistants (PAs)** — Targeting physicians is a bit old school. But, it still works well for many firms due to the decent earning potential and their desire to outsource their financial lives since the work schedule is so hectic. Although the income potential may not be as high, there are some specialty Physician Assistants (PA) out there that earn more than primary care physicians/general practitioners, and they are typically much younger since PA school is only two years. The same goes for Nurse Practitioners as well who have stable, long-term, high-paying jobs that the profession over-

---

4. "Blue Ocean Strategy & Blue Ocean Shift: Create Blue Oceans of New Market Space," Blue Ocean Strategy, accessed February 18, 2022, https://www.blueoceanstrategy.com/.

looks in favor of physicians.

- **Social Media Influencers** — The proliferation of social media platforms has created an entire subset of new entrepreneurs who can make tens of millions of dollars per year making funny videos of themselves. These people are generally young and in dire need of someone to help manage their affairs and protect them from themselves at times and their entourages.

- **Professors** — Income is limited to mid-six figures at the most. However, their situations are usually not overly complicated; they have substantial benefits and retirement packages. Like doctors, they are highly educated in other fields outside of financial planning and have long, steady, stable careers. The challenge with this group, as well as any other highly educated profession, is that they think they can do it on their own. They are more prone to be do it yourselfers or validators who want to make the decision and only be validated that it is the right one versus delegators which I think are the best types of clients because once the trust is built up, they turn over everything to their financial planner.

- **Software Engineers** — It seems like every recruiter in the entire country is trying to recruit software engineers because the demand for this skillset is very high. This group's income potential has risen rapidly and can easily be in the low six figures with only a few years of experience. Established financial planners are generally targeting the VP or Manager level executives who are several levels above.

If you are asking yourself how you might meet these types of people, you do need to develop a marketing strategy which is beyond the scope of this book. But a good place to start to meet these types of people is to get out and live your life. One financial planner I know well has had a lot of success meeting high-net-worth individuals in the adoption and foster care community, the adventure race/trail running community, and the cycling community, to name a few.

Let's wrap things up with a few ideas and tips on developing and honing your firm management skills.

Developing and Honing Your Firm Management Skills

Whether you decide to go down the managerial focus career track, you need to develop management skills because managing people is much more than telling others what to do. Since few have the talent to manage effectively, for most people to become effective in this area of their career, they must either outsource it or put in a lot of hard work, practice, and secure some additional education to do it effectively.

As your career progresses, you might find yourself in charge of several support staff ranging from client service people, interns, and associate planners. And you may not have the desire or ability to secure additional education, such as an MBA, that can help with these areas.

So, in lieu of a massive investment of time and money into your career, here are some tips for you to consider when you find yourself needing to manage people:

Tip #1 — Remember where you came from

If a management role came through internal promotion, you have built-in credibility, as your team has likely seen you in action. It can also be a motivational play for them, as they have seen someone excel and be rewarded. Some may try to abuse this, though, and not follow your directions. In these cases, set clear expectations and firm boundaries.

Also, remember to be respectful of those who helped you get there. Far too many times, excess tension is caused by managers alienating the very people that helped them get to where they are. On the flip side, be sure not to swing the other way as many politicians do in rewarding only those that have assisted their climb to power.

One of the best managers I ever had was one of my peers at a job I had during college. I knew where he came from, and he never tried to abuse his position, but he did make it clear that he was now in charge, which we respected because he was a tireless worker.

Also, be careful about shaking things up all at once. Some changes may need to be made, but remember people dislike change, and this can cause resentment from the outset, especially if it is an overwhelming amount.

Tip #2 — Clear and open communication channels

Whether you receive an internal or external promotion, schedule one-on-one lunch meetings with your new team members. This gives you a chance to listen to them and learn what they are seeking from their careers.

These interactions also help you discern how best to manage them. Just like dealing with clients, you might have to adjust your style slightly depending on the situation and who it involves. But they will appreciate the opportunity to tell you about themselves privately.

Finally, emphasize teamwork and collaboration. Many of the financial planning firm clients we recruit for at New Planner Recruiting that are experiencing the greatest growth, and employee satisfaction have moved beyond the vertical military-type management structure and have replaced it with a more horizontal system.

Tip #3 — Dealing with people that were passed over

When promotions are made, emotions run high, resentment can build, and you can find yourself railroaded quickly by someone who was passed over. Let's face it, no matter how good a manager or communicator you are, there will always be dissenters.

Ironically, dissension can make for a healthy organization, if not too excessive. But you must be able to deal with it effectively. When I have worked with and had to manage people that thought they should have been in my spot, I found going directly to them and being honest about the delicate situation goes a long way to rebuilding a solid working relationship.

Even something as simple as saying, "*I know you were hoping for the Lead Advisor position and were disappointed when they named me. I have worked hard just like you, and I did not ask for this, but I do feel I deserve it and am ready for the challenge of making this the best team in the firm. I know it is awkward, but I hope this doesn't cause a rift between us because we have a lot of work to do and must make the best of the situation. Thanks for letting me share that. How are you feeling about this?*"

Tip #4—Connecting with prior generations

These could likely be people in other areas of the business, and you could find yourself promoted to something like Director of Financial Planning, where you might have other more Senior Financial Advisors who are reporting to you. Consider asking them for feedback, which lets them know they have a voice, and you are respecting them rather than abusing your position and power.

Also, since they place significant emphasis on seniority and can be workaholics, consider putting in some extra hours so you happen to be around when they show up and leave each day.

Tip #5 — Develop your style

Even having loathed managers for years, some new managers will try to copy their boss's management style, even if subconsciously. This can be a mistake if it doesn't represent your style, and it can create the impression you are a placeholder puppet for senior management.

Think of Roger Daltrey's words in The Who's hit song *Won't Get Fooled Again:* "Meet the new boss, same as the old boss!" Besides, what worked for the prior boss might not work for you. Reach out to all the mentors you have developed due to my harping! Their wisdom and guidance, combined with your own experiences, should get you most of the way.

Be wary of the temptation to take credit for everything or to start micromanaging. This tends to happen when new managers think they need to prove themselves. Remember, employees are less likely to work hard for a manager who takes credit for everything, is a know-it-all, micromanages, and delegates work that they would not do themselves.

So, keep these tips in mind during your decision-making process. Just like in parenting, developing your style may take years to develop.

***

If you end up joining a large organization, they will probably already have dedicated professional management taking care of these functions so you can solely focus on your core competencies. But you must realize that it will be tough for you to ascend to any type of partnership role if you cannot manage people, at least at a basic level.

So, you should now be on track for deliberate and consistent skill development in all areas of the four-legged stool: technical, relational, sales, and firm management. Keep in mind that these are major areas of learning and growth that will not be mastered overnight. So be patient and work hard and continue to move forward!

Finally, here are a few closing thoughts for you to keep in mind throughout the remainder of your career.

Don't compare yourself to others.

It is the same concept you tell your clients when they try to keep up with the Joneses. You don't know the other person's situation. This is hard to do, but you will waste a lot of time and become depressed if you are overly worried about others in a similar position.

Be aware but not focused on your competition.

The famous saying is, "Obsess about your clients, not about your competition." If you continue to increase your skill set, innovate, and provide value to your clients, you will be successful.

Manage your resources wisely.

Time is your most precious resource, so protect it in any way you can. The earlier in your career you can find the one or two things you are good at, the quicker you will reach your goals. Remember, you can always make more money, but you cannot make more time.

Exhibit patience.

Realize that successful careers and businesses take decades to build. Contrary to our culture, it is okay to take the long game and not receive instant gratification. You should also expect to have setbacks and failures along the way. As much as you might want your career to look like a neat smooth lineup and to the right, it probably will not happen that way. Be flexible and understand you might have to take a step back to take several steps forward.

Key Takeaways

- You have a lot of opportunities, and there are exciting times ahead for you.

- This career isn't just about sales.

- Dealing with people and getting them to do what you want them to do is difficult, and you will need to practice.

- The founding generation developed their careers much differently than you will.

Action Items

- Review Chapter 13 Materials using this QR Code.

- Think about your skill set and what area you think would be most satisfied: Technical, Relational, or Managerial. Ask yourself - do I enjoy managing/leading people? Digging into the IRS tax code when everyone else is watching the super bowl? Meeting every single person at a networking event?

- Write down 2–3 things that you think set apart a good planner from a great planner.

CONCLUSION

I hope it was as much fun to learn about how you can enter and succeed in the financial planning profession and the endless opportunities it provides for you as much as I enjoyed writing about it. Based on thousands of conversations I have had over the years with people in other career fields, you truly cannot find a better profession out there—people in lots of different industries (that seem very exciting and well paying) want to join financial planning!

You now have the blueprint for success starting as a financial planner. There will always be hiccups and gotcha-type moments along the way, but you now have the knowledge and experience for what to expect and how to navigate your way to ultimate career success.

Just like my high school basketball coach told me when I couldn't quite dunk a basketball, "If it was easy, everyone could do it!!" Becoming a great financial planner is not easy; however, I think you will find it was worth all the effort and sacrifices you may have to make in the end.

Remember to be grateful that you have this opportunity to join such a wonderful profession and that you found out about it when you did versus years from now. Now, go, feeling well equipped and remember to pay it forward and not keep this terrific profession a secret, but always speak about the numerous ways it impacts our global community.

Resources

Here is the QR code we mentioned at the beginning of the book. Scan the code for an easy way to access all of the graphs, charts, tables, examples, and additional resources, such as our Salary Reports that we update periodically. Make sure you check back from time to time and/or sign up for our newsletter list so you will be notified when new resources are added to the portal.

Works Cited

"12 Tribes of Financial Planning Career Resource." *Financial Advisor Magazine*, Financial Advisor Magazine, https://www.fa-mag.com/userfiles/2019_FA_Online/Expert_Views/Screen_Shot_2019-06-26_at_11.35.19_AM-chart1.png. Accessed 19 Apr. 2023.

"About the CFP Exam." *About the CFP Exam | CFP Board*, https://www.cfp.net/get-certified/certification-process/exam-requirement/about-the-cfp-exam.

"Advancing Knowledge in Financial Planning." *Nerd's Eye View | Kitces.com*, 21 Mar. 2023, http://www.kitces.com/.

"Amplified Planning." *Amplified Planning*, https://amplifiedplanning.com/.

"Behavioral Finance." *Coursera*, https://www.coursera.org/learn/duke-behavioral-finance.

"Blue Ocean Strategy & Blue Ocean Shift: Create Blue Oceans of New Market Space." *Blue Ocean Strategy*, 21 Apr. 2023, https://www.blueoceanstrategy.com/.

"Blx Internship Program." *BLX Internship*, https://blxinternship.org/.

"Caleb Brown, MBA, CFP® - Co-Founder - Planning Zoo | Linkedin." *LinkedIn*, https://www.linkedin.com/in/calebbrowncfp.

"CFP Board." *CFP Board | Certified Financial Planner Board of Standards, Inc.*, http://www.cfp.net/.

"CFP® Exam: What You'll Be Tested On." *CFP® Exam: What You'll Be Tested On | CFP Board*, https://www.cfp.net/get-certified/certification-process/exam-requirement/about-the-cfp-exam/what-youll-be-tested-on.

Dore, Kate. "Are You Prepared for Tax Impact of the $68 Trillion Great Wealth Transfer? Here Are Some Options to Reduce the Bite." *CNBC.com*, 12 July 2021, Are you prepared for tax impact of the $68 trillion great wealth transfer? Here are some options to reduce the bite.

"Financial Life Planning: Financial Advisor Coaching." *Mitch Anthony*, 23 Feb. 2023, https://www.mitchanthony.com/.

"Find a Broker, Investment or Financial Advisor." *BrokerCheck*, https://brokercheck.finra.org/.

"FPA Membership." *Financial Planning Association*, https://www.financialplanningassociation.org/membership.

Gallup, Inc. "Cliftonstrengths." *Gallup.com*, Gallup, 10 Apr. 2023, http://www.gallup.com/cliftonstrengths/en/home.aspx.

"Home Page." *Money Quotient*, 15 Mar. 2023, https://www.moneyquotient.com/.

"Home Page." *Paragon Resources, Inc.*, https://www.paragonresources.com/.

"Home Page." *Sperling's Best Places - Data Sources*, https://www.bestplaces.net/docs/datasource.aspx.

"Human Skills Institute™ – Effective Action for Meaningful Growth ..." *Human Skills Institute*, https://humanskillsinstitute.com/.

"IAPD - Investment Adviser Public Disclosure - Homepage." *IAPD - Investment Adviser Public Disclosure - Homepage*, https://adviserinfo.sec.gov/.

"Kinder Institute of Life Planning." *Kinder Institute of Life Planning ' Financial Life Planning Starts Here*, https://www.kinderinstitute.com/.

"Life Is Change. Be Prepared." *Sudden Money Institute*, https://www.suddenmoney.com/.

The Myers & Briggs Foundation, https://www.myersbriggs.org/.

"The National Association of Personal Financial Advisors." *The National Association of Professional Financial Advisors*, https://www.napfa.org/membership.

"Newplannerrecruiting.com." *New Planner Recruiting*, https://newplannerrecruiting.com/.

"Personal Financial Advisors: Occupational Outlook Handbook." *U.S. Bureau of Labor Statistics*, U.S. Bureau of Labor Statistics, 8 Sept. 2022, https://www.bls.gov/ooh/business-and-financial/personal-financial-advisors.htm.

Planning Zoo. "Planning Zoo." *Planning Zoo*, https://planningzoo.com/.

"Professional Designations." *Professional Designations | FINRA.org*, https://www.finra.org/investors/professional-designations.

Published by Statista Research Department, and Sep 22. "Number of Rias Employed in the U.S. 2021." *Statista*, 22 Sept. 2022, https://www.statista.com/statistics/614815/number-of-rias-employed-usa/.

Salinger, Tobias. "17,500 State-Registered Rias to Get Fee Guidance from Nasaa." *Financial Planning*, Financial Planning, 28 May 2021, https://www.financial-planning.com/news/state-registered-rias-to-get-fee-guidance-from-nasaa.

"Securities Industry Essentials® (SIE®) Exam." *Securities Industry Essentials® (SIE®) Exam | FINRA.org*, https://www.finra.org/registration-exams-ce/qualification-exams/securities-industry-essentials-exam.

"Series 65 – Uniform Investment Adviser Law Exam." *Series 65 – Uniform Investment Adviser Law Exam | FINRA.org*, https://www.finra.org/registration-exams-ce/qualification-exams/series65.

"Study Material Vendors." *NASAA*, https://www.nasaa.org/exams/study-material-vendors.

"Type Descriptions." *The Enneagram Institute*, https://www.en neagraminstitute.com/type-descriptions/.

"Verify a CFP® Professional." *Verify a CFP® Professional | CFP Board*, https://www.cfp.net/verify-a-cfp-professional.

— • —

ACKNOWLEDGEMENTS

I have been working on this book ever since I began my financial planning career almost 20 years ago. When I finally began the formal writing process, the Coronavirus Pandemic of 2020 hit and temporarily interrupted the project, and it did take me some time to get back on track. I am so grateful for my family, friends, and colleagues who have helped me along the way.

Starting with my spouse, Jenny, a brilliant professor and writer, who I can run anything by and immediately become unstuck. You are truly better than I deserve. My children, Gracie and Graylan, who continue to motivate and inspire me.

The team at New Planner Recruiting—you guys are wonderful, and we have so much fun together. Thanks for dealing with me when I get stressed and for helping shape the company that it is today allowing us to impact the financial planning profession for many generations to come.

My colleagues in the CEO Study Group: Erin Kincheloe and Sue Chesney for reviewing the early drafts and helping me plan out the flow of the chapters and for holding me accountable when the last thing I wanted to do was review and correct edits.

My friends Lindsay Elwood, Joe Goetz, and Paul Brown, who have spent a lot of time with me over the years and helped me stay focused and positive.

Deanna Brown, my stepmother, who changed the trajectory of my life in so many good ways and for your keen eye when editing my grammar and spelling mistakes.

Yuki Kobayashi and Ryan Grava, two of my students at the University of Georgia's Financial Planning Program, who read an early manuscript and gave me some great feedback. I am thankful for the time I get to spend each spring learning about and from the next generation of financial planners.

Michael Kitces, my friend and business partner, for helping me develop a clear vision for the audience and not stray from it no matter how hard I tried to.

About the Author

Caleb is the host of the New Planner Podcast, Co-founder and CEO of New Planner Recruiting. This recruiting firm specializes in sourcing, screening, and integrating financial planners in financial planning firms nationwide. He was named the Next Generation Influencer by Financial Planning magazine, one of the top 25 most influential people in the industry by Investment Advisor, and Investment News 40 under 40. He is a graduate of the Texas Tech Personal Financial Planning Program and started his career spending over five years in an RIA firm in North Texas, helping a sole practitioner transition the firm to an ensemble model. He has been recognized as a Distinguished Alumnus for the TTU College of Human Sciences as well as a Distinguished Alumnus for the TTU Financial Planning Program. His book *Successful Hiring for Financial Planners: The Human Capital Advantage* is a compilation of the to-do's and what not to do's in hiring for a financial planning firm so business owners can alleviate pain points often associated with hiring.

He is a Kolbe Certified™ Consultant and original creator of the FPA Career Day program, which began with the Dallas/ Ft. Worth chapter and subsequently has been implemented by other organizations across the nation. Throughout Brown's career, he has mentored, hired, managed, and coached many career changers and college students seeking internships and full-time positions in financial planning, as well as the firm owners who hire them. He is also an Adjunct Faculty member of the University of Georgia's Financial Planning Program. Recently he co-founded Planning Zoo, which was established to assist advisors in data entry services while teaching financial planning students how to do "real planning."

Outside of work, Caleb coaches youth sports and volunteers with various programs benefiting foster and adoptive kids. He is also an avid golfer, hiker, Tough Mudder, and snowboarder.

41205955R00120